AirTight

AirTight

Security Solutions for the New Millennium

Clint Kirkwood

WestBow
PRESS
A DIVISION OF THOMAS NELSON

WestBow Press books may be ordered through booksellers or by contacting:

WestBow Press
A Division of Thomas Nelson
1663 Liberty Drive
Bloomington, IN 47403
www.westbowpress.com
1-(866) 928-1240

Because of the dynamic nature of the Internet, any web addresses or links contained in this book may have changed since publication and may no longer be valid. The views expressed in this work are solely those of the author and do not necessarily reflect the views of the publisher, and the publisher hereby disclaims any responsibility for them.

Any people depicted in stock imagery provided by Thinkstock are models, and such images are being used for illustrative purposes only.

Certain stock imagery © Thinkstock.

ISBN: 978-1-4497-4842-5 (sc)

Library of Congress Control Number: 2012908539

Printed in the United States of America

WestBow Press rev. date: 06/21/2012

DEDICATION

To my beautiful wife, Myrah, who inspires me to be forever young. Without your love and patience, life would not be the adventure it is and remains today. You are a treasure, and I will love you until the moon is no more!

Moreover, to my sister and brother-in-law, Sharon and Allen May, who so clearly demonstrate the real meaning of BFFs. Myrah and I will never forget you two.

Clint (June bug)

TABLE OF CONTENTS

List of Illustrations

List of Tables

PREFACE

After teaching security and criminal justice courses at several high schools, colleges and career schools, I was surprised to learn that the majority of students were not informed regarding the role of security professionals within the security industry. I can recall during numerous class sessions that even though there were many inquiries regarding criminology, parole and policing, there were four particular questions that drew the most concern; 1) how to conduct a security survey; 2) how to identify certain characteristics of those who would likely be involved in workplace violence; 3) what are the proper procedures for responding to emergencies at schools, colleges and universities, and; 4) how to establish an effective executive protection or VIP program.

Therefore, I saw a need to provide a resource that would adequately address the aforementioned questions, as well as provide a method by which to teach the material. This handbook was ultimately developed to address key security concepts, i.e., Crime Prevention Through Environmental Design or CPTED (pronounced sep-ted), Guidelines for Combating Workplace Violence, a Guide for School Safety and Security, and Executive Protection, and finally, provide a useful reference for the law enforcement and security professionals of the future.

1 INTRODUCTION

As the culture grows increasingly impersonal, individuals are concerned with personal safety and the protection of personal property more than ever before. Likewise, public safety is considered one of the top priorities of the government, though; this trend may be due in part to the terrorist attacks of September 2001. Recent studies revealed that approximately $44 billion dollars per year is spent on public emergency services, including police and fire, and approximately $104 billion dollars is spent in the private sector (the Hallcrest Report II), on similar services. Even as individuals are investing significant resources to protect themselves physically and materially, similarly, businesses are realizing that investing in an effective security program can ultimately protect the bottom line.

Unfortunately, we live with the elements of crime and criminal behavior every day as a fact of life. Early practitioners focused more on the apprehension and punishment of the offender (which often times cannot be initiated until a crime has already been committed), rather than the implementation of crime prevention measures. Crime prevention is a service function and when properly executed, has tremendous impact. In as much as its value may be difficult to measure or quantify, the impact of crime prevention may be determined more appropriately by what does not happen, rather than by what does (Sennewald, 2003). However, experience dictates that large segments of the society think of crime prevention in terms of target hardening (traditional security measures), but there are other advanced practicable options to consider.

Crime Prevention Through Environmental Design (CPTED), is an extraordinary approach to reducing and preventing crime, and should be factored into any new construction, and considered for retrofit of existing construction. Far more advanced than just hardware, as in mechanical locking devices or barricades, the CPTED principles of crime prevention are applied with less difficulty and cost during the **design phase** of a project. Typically, once an architect is commissioned to design the facility, it is at this stage when it is imperative for security leadership to become involved to ensure that the infrastructure will be in place for planned security technology and upgrades.

Just as specific guidelines that point to aesthetics and functionality are designed into the project, security features must have the same consideration. Once the design has been completed and accepted by the owner, introducing major changes after the fact become not only difficult but also costly. Security professionals should not assume that security measures would be considered at the design stage, but rather assume they will not. Traditionally, architectural firms do not specialize in projects with major security overtones, so it is not only imperative of security leadership to get involved as stated earlier, but it is also a responsibility.

In terms of best practices, design professionals have historically integrated features into architectural drawings that serve as resistance to natural threats such as tornadoes, earthquakes, fires, extreme temperatures and floods, depending upon the geographical location. In recent years as the CPTED concept has become more understood and its value more appreciated, security professionals have been included at the facility planning stage to ensure that effective security is incorporated into the overall layout and scheme of the project.

What is more, design professionals have begun to recognize crime as a man-made hazard that can be resisted through quality design systems, and as a result of the latter, planned communities in Virginia, St. Louis, Chicago, Detroit and Macon, as well as in the UK, have recorded significant successes with regard to crime reduction and prevention. The National Crime Prevention Institute indicated the following regarding the use of CPTED strategies: "*The proper design and effective use of the built environment can lead to a reduction in the fear and incidence of crime, and an improvement of the quality of life…*"

Architectual drawing

The design and characteristics of a particular space will determine how it is used. For instance, a large room with a flat concrete floor, may attract skate boarders, or a building with no windows, may attract illicit drug activity. Modern CPTED must consider environmental criminological issues that influence opportunities for unwanted activity and up to criminal activity at specific locations. Therefore, to provide a simple guide for determining the appropriateness of space design and usage, the approach should include the **Definition, Design** and **Designation** methods (Sorensen, 2000).

Space Definition requires that the following questions be considered: Is it clear who owns and manages it? Where are its natural borders? Are there cultural or social definitions that effect how the space is used? Are there symbolic signs? Is there a misconception or conflict between the designated purpose and definition?

Space Design requires that the following questions be considered: Can the **"Defensible Space"** approach be utilized (**public, semi-public, semi-private and private**)? How well does the physical design support the intended use? How well does the physical design support the definition of the behavior most desired? Does the physical design conflict with the way in which the use of the space will be most productive (Newman, 1976)?

DEFENSIBLE SPACE

Defensible space

Space ownership – defined

2 CPTED PRINCIPLES IN ACTION

CPTED design strategies have been around for decades; however, urban planning experts successfully explored the relationship between the built environment and criminal behavior. A close assessment and subsequent implementation of the following strategies will provide guidelines that property owners, developers and design professionals may apply to reduce the fear and incidence of crime, and thereby improving the quality of life.

Four (4) related CPTED strategies will be utilized to complete the assessment. They include Natural Access Control, Natural Surveillance, Territorial Reinforcement and Maintenance.

Crime prevention through proper maintenance

NATURAL ACCESS CONTROL

Natural Access Control is a concept directed largely at decreasing the opportunity to commit a crime by denying access to crime targets, and creating a perception of risk associated with crime for the offenders. Properly located and utilized entrances, exits, fencing, landscaping and lighting, can direct both human and vehicular traffic in a way that discourages crime or conflict and enhances the natural use of the property. Proper planning or use of property at the design stage, and/or with existing property, can influence how visitors and residents use the property. The elements of design are very useful tools to plainly indicate public routes and discourage access to private areas, and can affect the second CPTED strategy – NATURAL SURVEILLANCE.

Proper access – one-way in, one-way out

NATURAL SURVEILLANCE

"Abnormal" users do not wish to be seen or noticed. Placing physical features, activities and people in a way that maximizes the ability to identify and observe an area while keeping intruders recognizable, will discourage crime. In addition, "normal" users of the space feel more comfortable in the area since they are able to observe others using the space.

Examples of features that will maximize the visibility of the wrongdoer are unobstructed doors and windows, pedestrian-friendly streets and walkways, the use of porches, and the utilization of appropriate lighting at night. Poorly planned barriers such as hedges, shadows, building corners, improperly located dumpsters, privacy fences and so forth, make it difficult to observe activity. Landscaping and lighting can be planned or maintained to promote natural surveillance from inside the residential or office environment, and the approach to the property. Maximizing the natural surveillance of "gatekeepers", such as neighboring residents, security personnel and other workers, can deter abnormal use of the property. This enticement to naturally observe the general environment can also positively promote the third CPTED strategy – TERRITORIAL REINFORCEMENT.

Proper usage of natural surveillance

TERRITORIAL REINFORCEMENT

People generally protect territory that they feel belongs to them and have a certain respect for the territory of others. The concept of territorial reinforcement concentrates on features that define property lines with the aim of distinguishing between private and public spaces. Territory is established with the use of fences, open-fences, pavement and gateway treatments, floor and wall treatments, art, and appropriate signs and landscaping, which are some of the tangible ways in which to express ownership or encourage users to care for the area. Identifying intruders, or other abnormal users of the space, is straightforward in an environment that is "owned" by normal users of the property or space.

When fencing is installed to define property lines, it is best to use a seven-foot high straight bar tubular steel fence. This type of fencing will deter graffiti, provide an attractive feature and not obstruct common observation. Signs are usually placed on boundary fencing, typically, at 50-foot intervals, to indicate ownership and to alert of possible danger inside. If there were a need to fence a large area, chain link can be used to mark boundaries or discourage penetration by small animals. When addressing animals, the height of the fence can be four feet. On the other hand, a chain link fence intended to discourage human penetration is generally not less than seven feet in height, and depending upon the circumstances, a top guard of barbed wire (one-foot), can be added. In addition, the actual method used when installing fencing is very important and items such as posts, fence tops and gates should be properly gauged.

Posts – terminal posts are placed at the ends and corners of fences and used to support gates. Pull-posts are terminal posts bracing a long stretch of fence or offering a change of elevation. All other posts are line-posts. Line-posts should be spaced at equal distant intervals not to exceed 10 feet on the average when measured from center to center between posts and parallel to the fence grade. Under normal conditions, the diameter of the postholes should be four times the largest cross section of the post, but local conditions may indicate the post footing dimensions. The depth of the posthole should be a minimum of 24 inches (609.6 mm), plus an additional three inches (76.2 mm) for each foot (305 mm) increase in height over four feet (1.22 m). After the post has been set plumb and in line, the hole should be backfilled with concrete (2500 psi), and the exposed surface of the concrete crowned to shed water.

The fence fabric should be No. 9 A.W.G. or heavier, and the mesh openings should not be larger than two inches (50 mm). On fences, five feet (1,524 mm) high and under, selvage should be knuckled at both ends. On fences higher than five feet, selvage should be knuckled at one end and twisted at the other. On fences with less than two-inch mesh, all selvages should be knuckled. Fabric should be stretched taut approximately two inches above ground or paving, and securely fastened to the posts. Three strands of barbed wire fence tops are generally spaced six inches (152.4 mm) apart. Wooden fences are not normally recommended due to the high cost of repairs and graffiti removal.

Signage should be placed at the entrance and along the fence line. The signs should read – "No Loitering or Trespassing", and indicate a warning such as, "All violators will be prosecuted by the concerned jurisdiction." All signage and fencing should be well kept and maintenance completed promptly.

Proper chain-link fence structure

Proper chain-link fence structure

In addition, normal users contribute to the overall up-keep of the property, influencing the fourth CPTED strategy – MAINTENANCE.

MAINTENANCE

An important study called the "Broken Window Theory", has shown that the condition of the property can influence the way in which people visually interpret the overall culture and attitude of the normal users of the space. The theory proved that property in poor condition and lacking in repairs sends the message that no one cares about the property or the activity being supported. This message invites abnormal users to find comfort in the fact that their presence and activity will likely go unnoticed. Well-maintained property and space boldly announce that the users care for the surroundings and are more likely to notice undesired use and behavior.

Broken window theory

High quality maintenance and the overall condition of the property should be a priority since it delivers a continuous positive message to users, visitors and workers, while discouraging the abnormal user from abusing the space. Proper maintenance also guards against reduced visibility due to plant overgrowth and foiled or inoperative lighting, while serving as an added face of territoriality and ownership. Conversely, inappropriate maintenance such as over pruned hedges and shrubs can prevent landscape rudiments from achieving the desired outcomes, and care must be taken to communicate unambiguous design intent to maintenance personnel.

Proper maintenance of greenery

CPTED emphasizes natural use of the environment to achieve security benefits. After exhausting the natural use of the environment, secondary measures to strengthen the effectiveness of the strategy can be used. These secondary measures are usually mechanical devices such as locking, lighting and electronics, organized security guards and patrols, and procedural policies and habitual practices. When these measures are used, they tend to be more effective in an environment that has been designed to support the use of countermeasures. It then becomes very important to adequately maintain these countermeasures to ensure that they are operational and contribute to their original intended function.

Home displays proper night-lighting techniques

3 CPTED STRATEGIES/TECHNIQUES

RESIDENTIAL DISTRICT

The safety measures employed in newly developed residential districts, such as high walls, gates, fencing, fortified doors and windows, and closed circuit television (CCTV) monitored entrances, can sometimes project that there is a crime problem in the area, having a negative effect on the local residents. In other words, the presence of security devices can imply that crime and the potential for criminal activity do exist. The implementation of CPTED strategies in residential neighborhoods can help create a safer environment and one in which criminal activity is difficult to carry out, all without sacrificing aesthetics.

By using techniques such as designing streets with gateway treatments, narrowing center-islands, roundabouts, traffic circles, neck downs, raised crosswalks, decorative and colored asphalts, speed bumps, and other traffic-calming devices, designers can establish territory and discourage speeding and cut-through traffic. Also by keeping public areas highly discernible, a message is sent to potential offenders that the risk of committing a crime is far too high. Criminals prefer low-risk situations requiring the least amount of effort on their part, and typically avoid situations where there is high visibility, which increases the potential for apprehension.

Gateway treatment

Traffic calming intersection

The following are simple cost effective measures, which will have a much more positive effect on residents than intimidating security devices.

NATURAL ACCESS CONTROL

❖ Limit access without completely disconnecting the development from other sub-divisions, and residential districts.

❖ Design streets to discourage pedestrian cut-through or vehicular high-speed traffic.

❖ Install paving treatments, plantings and architectural design features such as columned gateways and traffic calming features, to guide visitors to desired entrances and away from private areas.

❖ Install walkways in locations that are safe for pedestrians, and keep them unobstructed with proper maintenance.

❖ Install "shrubbery fences" as a feature to control pedestrian traffic.

❖ Use greenery to define areas surrounding individual properties (gardens, flowers, bushes).

NATURAL SURVEILLANCE

❖ Do not install landscaping that can create blind spots or hiding places.

❖ Keep bushes and other greenery pruned.

❖ Design "defensible space" (space that is marked as their own by gardens, landscaping and see-through fencing).

❖ Adequately illuminate physical obstructions.

❖ Centrally locate open spaces, open parks and recreational areas, to be visible from nearby streets and homes.

❖ Use pedestrian scale street lighting in high pedestrian traffic areas to assist the residents in identifying potential threats afterhours or when visibility is reduced.

❖ Sponsor get-acquainted activities to allow the neighbors to become familiar with each other.

❖ Alter non see-through fencing, barriers, and garbage receptacles.
❖ Create resident patrols.

Centrally located greenery and recreational area

TERRITORIAL REINFORCEMENT

❖ Design streets, facilities, and homes to encourage interaction between neighbors.
❖ Highlight entrances with the name of the development using gateway treatments; different paving materials, changes in street elevation, architectural and landscape designs.
❖ Plainly label homes with street address numbers that are a minimum of three inches high and made of reflective substances for night viewing.
❖ Define property lines with post and pillar type fencing, gates, and greenery to direct pedestrian traffic to the preferred points of admittance.

- ❖ Provide sufficient clear area from the perimeter to the building wall to prevent unauthorized access on foot or vehicle, without being observed.
- ❖ Display property signs to identify ownership of property (no trespassing, no solicitors, etc.).
- ❖ Surprisingly, dogs can serve as natural territorial reinforcement.

MAINTENANCE

- ❖ Hold all universal areas to very high standards, including entrances, right of ways, and boulevards.
- ❖ Put into effect deed restrictions and agreements, in addition to all city and county codes.
- ❖ Establish a "hot-line" for emergency repairs.
- ❖ Establish open lines of communication with the Department of Public Works.
- ❖ Immediately report failed conditions with public lighting, barriers, graffiti, or other perimeter problems.

SINGLE FAMILY DWELLINGS

Healthy communities are central to the wellbeing of families, and the interaction of its members creates support and security. Housing and environments can be designed to promote interaction between neighbors, however in many neighborhoods, the installation of gates and fences between homes create barriers and send a message of isolation, discouraging contact. In the past, front porches were prevalent, and naturally functioned as a gathering spot making neighbors more visible to each other. Over time, front porches gave way to tall privacy gates and fencing, and priority was given to increasing interior living space, causing neighbors to see each other less. However, when neighbors see each other, they tend to become more personally involved, and personal involvement creates a sense of caring and a desire to protect, which is exactly the point of the overall CPTED strategy. The photograph below illustrates the use of low bushes, hedges and shrubbery rather than high fencing, which makes it easier for neighbors to see each other and interact more freely.

Well-defined property

NATURAL ACCESS CONTROL

❖ Use walkways and landscaping to guide visitors to desired entrances and away from private areas.
❖ Use greenery to define private areas surrounding property lines.
❖ Install barriers and design paths, walkways, and roads, to divert prohibited users from entering private areas.

NATURAL SURVEILLANCE

❖ Make sure all doorways that open to the outside are properly illuminated.
❖ Make front doors visible from the street, and avoid hidden entrances.
❖ Install windows on all sides of the house to provide full visibility of the property perimeter.
❖ Provide proper illumination to sidewalks, driveways, and all areas of the property.
❖ The driveway should be visible from either the front or back door and at least one window assembly installed.
❖ Select and install appropriate landscaping (bushes, shrubs, and hedges) that will allow unobstructed views of vulnerable doors and windows from the street.
❖ Establish police-community involvement with local law enforcement.

TERRITORIAL REINFORCEMENT

❖ Use front porches or patios to create an intermediary area between the street and the dwelling.
❖ Define boundaries and private areas with greenery, pavement treatments, signage or fences.
❖ Use figurative and physical barriers.
❖ House address should be clearly visible from the street, at least three inches high, and made of reflective material for night visibility.

❖ Perimeter fence lines and gates should be kept clear of debris that causes obstruction.

MAINTENANCE

❖ To avoid obstruction, keep trees and shrubs trimmed back from the windows, doors, and walkways. Shrubs shall be trimmed to three feet and the lower branches of trees pruned up to seven feet, to maintain clear visibility.

❖ Use exterior lighting to illuminate the perimeter during night hours and maintain proper working order.

❖ Keep property free of litter and trash, and trim greenery to provide the appearance that someone is caring for the property.

❖ Keep the dwelling, all attached property, and devices in good repair.

Proper maintenance projects positive image of property

MULTI-FAMILY DWELLINGS AND COMPLEXES

Multi-family homes (duplexes, triplexes and apartment complexes) are a matter of practicality as the population increases and land availability decreases. Although all residential areas will have their share of safety and security issues, the multi-family dwelling model tends to complicate these concerns. One of the main issues is controlling visitors and unidentified persons roaming unescorted through common areas that are shared, such as hallways, laundry rooms, recreation facilities, elevators, and parking areas. These spaces present opportunities for crime and the need for crime prevention.

Moreover, it is important to note that multi-family dwellings do not necessarily correlate to multiple security issues; however, it is safe to say that the potential for issues certainly does exist because of the numbers. It is therefore recommended that building managers initiate opportunities for residents to get to know each other via interactive community events. When there are more "eyes on the street" to monitor activity, multi-family dwellers will definitely benefit, and safeness and the perception of safeness can be the end result.

NATURAL ACCESS CONTROL

❖ Ensure that balcony railings and patio enclosures are maintained at less than 3½', and avoid using solid materials.
❖ Define entrances to the site and all attached facilities with landscaping, architectural design or gateway treatments.
❖ Fence-in yards, pedestrian flows, and dead-end spaces.
❖ Install entry phones and other electronic access controls.
❖ Discourage loitering by non-residents, and enforce all occupancy provisions.
❖ Use automatic door closers with locking devices on all common building entrances.
❖ Provide adequate illumination in hallways, utility areas, and entrances.

- ❖ Provide each unit with a separate entryway that is clearly visible from the street.
- ❖ Limit multiple access points.
- ❖ Elevators and stairwells should be centrally located and have the ability to be viewed by other users of the property.
- ❖ Utilize visitor check-in booths.

NATURAL SURVEILLANCE

- ❖ All exterior doors should be made visible from the street and/or to the neighboring residents.
- ❖ Design windows on all four facades of the building to allow proper visibility.
- ❖ Properly illuminate parking areas and walkways near the building.
- ❖ Position recreation areas such as pools, tennis courts, clubhouses, and playgrounds that will be visible from unit windows and doors.
- ❖ Securely screen or properly conceal trash dumpsters, but avoid creating blind areas and locations that can hide them.
- ❖ Design elevators and stairwells in locations that are clearly visible from inside-doors and windows; and to be open and properly illuminated, being careful not to enclose them behind solid walls.
- ❖ Keep greenery no more than three feet high to avoid obstruction, and for clear visibility in at-risk areas.
- ❖ Greenery should be set back three yards from all paths.
- ❖ Locate buildings that will allow the windows and doors of individual units to be visible from neighboring units.
- ❖ Design parking areas to be visible from windows and doors.
- ❖ Ensure that parking spaces are assigned to all residents (adjacent to the unit), and identified with miscellaneous numbers, and not the residents' actual unit number. Parking spaces conspicuously marked will make unauthorized parking easier to identify and less likely to occur.
- ❖ Designate visitor-parking areas near the building.
- ❖ Use proper lighting at all doors that open to the outside.
- ❖ Centrally locate playgrounds where they are clearly visible from all units, but not directly adjacent to parking lots or streets.

- ❖ Use see-through picket or iron fencing to allow adequate visibility at all times.
- ❖ Initiate an apartment and/or neighborhood watch program.

Successful utilization of all CPTED concepts

TERRITORIAL REINFORCEMENT

- ❖ Define property lines with low growing ground cover.
- ❖ Locate hedges and bushes not more than three feet high.
- ❖ Highlight building entrances with architectural treatments, lighting and landscaped greenery.
- ❖ Properly identify all buildings and residential units with street numbers that are a minimum of three inches high and well illuminated during nightfall. Numbers can also be made of reflective material.
- ❖ Trim trees away from lights, and the lowest level of tree branches six feet or more above the ground.
- ❖ Trim shrubs, bushes, and branches to provide two feet to six feet clear space next to buildings, between buildings and parking areas, and along paths and sidewalks.
- ❖ Install individual locking mailboxes next to the appropriate residential units.

MAINTENANCE

- ❖ Keep all commons areas neat, clean, and trimmed, including entrances, rights of way and esplanades.
- ❖ All landscape and foliage shall be maintained so as not to obstruct a neighboring view.
- ❖ Install and maintain exterior lighting for nighttime illumination.
- ❖ Prohibit abandoned and inoperative vehicles, and "crime magnets."
- ❖ Locate and install alternative approved sites for graffiti.

INSTITUTIONAL ESTABLISHMENTS

Many security professionals agree that it is difficult to prevent criminal activity at schools, colleges, banks, libraries, churches, and other institutional establishments, because it is widely known that although most of these establishments are highly concerned with issues of safety, they place very little emphasis on implementing a systems approach to detect/impede/prevent aggressive or criminal behavior. Security need not be cost prohibitive, and could include simple strategies for increasing surveillance especially in a mall setting, like collaborating to vary the hours of operation at difference establishments, which would help to avoid isolation of any one. As discussed earlier in the book, the best case scenario whenever possible is to include CPTED strategies at the design stage of new construction, which will automatically increase the likelihood that the building design will lend itself to lively pedestrian activity.

High pedestrian traffic areas provide additional "eyes and ears"

NATURAL ACCESS CONTROL

* ❖ Clearly specify the main entry point at the design stage.
* ❖ Design separate parking locations for employees and visitors, and position them a distance away from busy streets and avenues.
* ❖ Construct limited entrances, exits, and parking areas, making them flush with the street.
* ❖ Require a "screening" location to ensure that residents and visitors meet entrance requirements.
* ❖ Include a guest sign-in, where guests are required to register with their resident hosts or require a display of identification prior to entry.
* ❖ Require wooden signs as opposed to metal. Metal signs encourage drive-by shootings because of the sound they make when struck.
* ❖ Ensure that all employees are familiar with the security system to avoid false alarms.

NATURAL SURVEILLANCE

* ❖ Locate bus stops near areas of safe activity, providing transparent shelters and proper lighting.
* ❖ Avoid constructing graffiti magnets, such as large blank walls that limit visibility.
* ❖ Use walls with windows, various architectural details or greenery.
* ❖ Do not cover entrance windows with obstructions that prevent employees from observing the outside.
* ❖ Cluster like-commercial establishments to promote high or low pedestrian density.
* ❖ Locate group congregation areas to positions that are observable by other offices or staff personnel.

TERRITORIAL REINFORCEMENT

- ❖ Design signage that is professionally sound with architectural details and completely visible.
- ❖ Anti-loitering rules should be clearly displayed.
- ❖ Clearly define who legitimately uses the space and mark the boundaries of the property.
- ❖ Provide sufficient space from the building to property perimeter, to prevent unauthorized access via foot or vehicle without being observed.
- ❖ Make common areas observable from different vantage points.
- ❖ Maintain parking lot surfaces free of potholes, cracks, and any other indicators of disrepair.
- ❖ Clearly mark parking spaces by painting lines and numbers for parking stalls, but do not identify owners by unit numbers.
- ❖ Install sufficient lighting to discern areas around the perimeter.

MAINTENANCE

- ❖ Remove graffiti within 24-hours.
- ❖ Keep hedges, bushes, and greenery trimmed and pruned so as not to obstruct the view of public areas.
- ❖ Immediately pickup garbage and litter.
- ❖ Adequately maintain and empty garbage receptacles.
- ❖ Dumpsters should not be hidden; passersby should be able to see them.
- ❖ Dumpsters and garbage receptacles must have secure lids.
- ❖ Encourage establishments to use tall outdoor lighting fixtures that are equipped with vandal resistant features.

PUBLIC HOUSING

Public housing is subsidized by the federal government, and was established to assist low-income families, but does not exclude singles, and senior citizens. Currently, there is a variety of public housing styles, ranging from single-family to condominiums. Even though construction of these units is locally handled by Public Housing Authority (PHA) or HUD offices, individual concerns by residents have been recorded throughout history regarding safety and security. In an effort to decrease crime and the fear of crime, while increasing the risk of apprehension for potential offenders, the following steps are recommended:

<u>NATURAL ACCESS CONTROL</u>

- ❖ Keep balcony railings and enclosures less than 42 inches high and avoid using opaque materials.
- ❖ Define entrances to the site and each parking location with landscaping, architectural design or gateway treatments.
- ❖ Fence-in yards, pedestrian flows, and dead-end spaces.
- ❖ Install entry phones and electronic access controls.
- ❖ Ensure that various camera angles are properly monitored.
- ❖ Discourage loitering by non-residents and enforce occupancy provisions.
- ❖ Use devices that automatically lock upon closing on all common building entrances.
- ❖ Provide adequate illumination in hallways.
- ❖ Ensure that normal and emergency exits are clearly marked.
- ❖ Provide each unit with a separate entryway that is visible from the street.
- ❖ Centrally locate elevators and stairwells that can be viewed by other users.
- ❖ Limit multiple access points.
- ❖ Include visitor check-in booths or telephonic devices.
- ❖ Ensure that housing authority recreational areas are not freely open to outsiders.
- ❖ Locate litterbins where people are likely to accumulate trash.
- ❖ Detached storage sheds or other buildings should be equipped with lockable windows and doors.

NATURAL SURVEILLANCE

- ❖ Design buildings so that the exterior doors are visible from the street or to neighboring units.
- ❖ Use proper lighting at all doors that open to the outside.
- ❖ Install windows on all facades of buildings to allow proper visibility.
- ❖ Assign parking spaces to residents marked with a miscellaneous number. This makes unauthorized parking easier to identify and less likely to occur.
- ❖ Designate visitor-parking areas for visitors and random callers.
- ❖ Make parking areas visible from windows and doors.
- ❖ Adequately illuminate parking areas and walkways.
- ❖ Position housing authority recreational areas to be visible through the doors and windows of each unit.
- ❖ Centrally locate play areas where they are clearly visible from residential units, but not directly adjacent to parking lots or streets.
- ❖ Screen or conceal dumpsters, but avoid creating blind spots and hiding places.
- ❖ Build elevators and stairwells in locations that are clearly visible from doors and windows.
- ❖ Construct elevators and stairwells to be open and well lit, not enclosed behind solid walls.
- ❖ Allow shrubbery to be no more than three feet high for clear visibility in vulnerable areas.
- ❖ Schedule periodic walk-through initiatives by housing authority staff, security personnel and/or administrators.

TERRITORIAL REINFORCEMENT

- ❖ Define property lines with low growing ground cover.
- ❖ Locate hedges and bushes not more than three feet high in designated areas of the buildings.
- ❖ Accentuate building entrances with architectural elements by lighting and landscaping.
- ❖ Clearly identify all buildings and residential units with street numbers that are a minimum of three inches high and well illuminated during night operation.

❖ Trim trees away from lights, and lowest tree branches six feet or more above the ground.

❖ Trim shrubs, bushes and branches to provide two feet to six feet clear space next to buildings, between buildings and parking areas, and along paths and sidewalks.

❖ Place individually locking mailboxes in an appropriate location at the building entrance.

❖ Cleary post a trespassing policy and intent to prosecute all violators.

MAINTENANCE

❖ Create and enforce maintenance standards for all common areas, including entrances, rights of way and esplanades.

❖ Prune greenery back from windows, doorways and walkways.

❖ Locate and maintain exterior lighting in constant working order.

❖ Strictly enforce rules regarding abandoned vehicles and other "crime magnets" that provide opportunities for crime.

❖ Locate alternative approved sites for graffiti.

❖ Repair damaged and/or vandalized housing units immediately.

❖ Initiate a vacancy reduction program to maintain unit occupancy.

Pueblo Del Sol public housing in Los Angeles, CA

COMMERCIAL STRUCTURES

Drive-through commercial facilities such as fast food, banks and automatic teller machines (ATMs), are more vulnerable to criminal activity than enclosed facilities, mainly because they are generally constructed in hidden locations, and are used during odd hours of the night. Patrons conducting transactions are also known to have available cash, making them noticeable crime targets. Therefore, visibility should be paramount when designing and determining the location of these facilities.

NATURAL SURVEILLANCE

- ❖ Structures should be located to face main thoroughfares.
- ❖ The ordering positions of all fast food facilities should be clearly visible from the interior of the store and from main thoroughfares.
- ❖ The structures should have adequate lighting at the locations where cash is deposited and received.
- ❖ There should be no barriers, walls, or fencing that can be used as cover for criminals or criminal activity. Avoid landscaping designs that can hinder the response time of emergency service professionals if dispatched.
- ❖ Develop a positive image to encourage investor and user confidence to increase "eyes and ears" at all establishments.

Neighboring business partnerships

Self-service bank facing main road

ATM well visible from main road

COMMERCIAL ESTABLISHMENTS

A successful marketplace is dependent upon the vibrancy of its neighborhoods. For neighborhoods to remain healthy and strong, its local businesses must be economically strong and safe places to patronize. It is imperative for businesses that CPTED guidelines be utilized when designing and constructing commercial properties, as the issue of safety is often cited as an important consideration in choosing to shop at one store over another. Therefore, the strategy of occupying spaces where customers and employees can keep each other in view not only adds to the feeling of being safe and secure, it also adds to the bottom line.

NATURAL ACCESS CONTROL

❖ Locate parking areas, bus stops, and events closer to areas of increased activity.

❖ Provide both front and rear vehicle access.

❖ Provide rear access for employees, visitors, and patrons to the interior of the building when rear parking is provided.

❖ Provide public telephones with dial-free connections to emergency service personnel.

❖ Provide benches and other seating equipment to encourage pedestrian flow in specific areas.

❖ Construct barriers to restrict access to areas that are not intended for public use.

❖ Plainly mark public thoroughfares and regulate non-employee access to private areas.

❖ Utilize signage to direct patrons and visitors to specific areas of the facility.

❖ To allow viewing from the outside, position cash counters and checkout locations to the front of commercial businesses.

❖ Prevent easy access to locations utilized by emergency service personnel (roof or fire escape) from ground level.

NATURAL SURVEILLANCE

❖ Remove large signs and other obstruction that can interfere with fully observing the facility.
❖ Design rear windows of the facility to face the parking areas.
❖ Install adequate lighting at front and rear perimeters.
❖ Recommend that businesses establish "safe shelters" for people who feel endangered while on the street.
❖ Interior displays should not obstruct visibility from the outside, (others should be able to see inside, especially the police).
❖ Initiate a "Business Watch" program for additional "eyes and ears" on the street.
❖ Design shipping and receiving areas to avoid creating hiding locations for employees, patrons, delivery personnel, and items that can be easily stolen.
❖ Coordinate hours of operations with neighboring businesses to avoid isolation of a single facility.
❖ Design public restrooms to be observable from the reception area.
❖ Place all entrances, exists, and checkouts under visual surveillance and electronic monitors.
❖ Concession machines and pay telephones should be in unobstructed view of the employees.
❖ If public phones are available, use call-out phones only.
❖ Fully illuminate interior spaces.
❖ Avoid situations where only one employee is present.

TERRITORIAL REINFORCEMENT

❖ Businesses should be identified by wall signs for those parking in the rear.
❖ Position parking areas so they are clearly visible from interior or exterior of the building, with lanes properly marked to establish parking boundaries.
❖ Define property boundaries with landscaping, hedges, low fences, and gates.
❖ Define building boundaries with easements, signage, and graphics.
❖ Use signage to define the behaviors desired within the respective areas.

- Post perimeter signage at all entrances at a minimum of 100-foot intervals.
- Define and construct separate areas for private and public use.
- Install protective covering above doors and windows such as awnings and canopies.

MAINTENANCE

- Keep building, fencing, landscaping, paths, and walkways clean, trimmed and in good repair.
- Keep parking areas free of litter and trash, and the surface in good repair.
- Maintain signage, displays, and building evacuation instructions in good condition.
- Keep greenery groomed, trimmed, and kept to minimum height near windows, gates, garages, and access roads.
- Keep dumpsters empty and visible from hidden solid walls.
- Keep fire escapes and emergency exits clear of obstructions.
- Keep exterior lighting adequate, operational, and maintained.
- Prohibit auto repairs, abandoned vehicles, oil spills, and other debris on the grounds.

Properly marked and maintained parking facility

MALLS/SHOPPING CENTERS

Shopping centers are expected to be securely controlled and safe places for shopping, entertainment and dining. However, they present enormous problems for those who are charged with safety and security of patrons and employees. The centers have an abundance of shoppers with cash, groups of youthful teens hanging out, and parking lots jam packed with vehicles. To manage the crowd, the activities around shopping centers, and parking areas, there should be a clear distinction between shoppers or potential shoppers, and non-shoppers who are looking to engage in criminal activity. Certain design qualities of shopping centers can encourage or discourage the non-shoppers; such as proper lighting, color scheme, presence of public transportation, parking facilities, false windows, and many others. It is therefore more important than ever for developers, remodelers, and designers to implement CPTED principles.

NATURAL ACCESS CONTROL

❖ Locate parking areas, bus stops, and events closer to areas of increased activity.

❖ Provide public telephones with dial-free connections to emergency service personnel.

❖ Provide benches and other seating equipment to encourage pedestrian flow in specific areas.

❖ Use portable barriers at locations of the mall that are not intended for the public.

❖ Plainly mark public thoroughfares and regulate non-employee access to private areas.

❖ Utilize signage to direct patrons and visitors to specific mall locations.

❖ Position cash counters and checkout locations towards the front of individual shops.

❖ Prevent easy access to locations utilized by emergency service personnel (roof or fire escape) from ground level.

❖ Mark entrances with landscaping, planters, architectural treatments, and proper signage.

❖ Conspicuously mark the boundaries between public and private spaces.
❖ Use landscaping and water features to divide the parking areas into smaller lots.
❖ Separate loading zones with designated delivery hours from public parking areas.
❖ Prevent unsecured access to roof tops from interior or adjacent structures, such as parking garages.

NATURAL SURVEILLANCE

❖ Attempt to prevent fortress style designing, which negatively affects parking.
❖ Attach display cases to dead walls, to market products and to reduce the effect of the fortress designs.
❖ Active displays with proper lighting and mannequins will attract attention and enforce natural surveillance.
❖ Install false windows and lighting panels.
❖ Design restroom entrances to be visible from the main areas.
❖ Design restroom entrances without doors that will hinder observations, and use adequate lighting for full illumination.
❖ Adequately illuminate parking perimeter during night hours.
❖ Use perpendicular parking rather than parallel, to provide greater visibility between vehicles.
❖ Parking for nighttime employees should be located near entrances.
❖ Design parking garages to provide visibility to all levels from the ground floor.
❖ Use quality lighting and bright paint when designing the garage areas.
❖ Avoid designing external walls without windows or openings.
❖ Use water-retention features that are visible from ground level, free of hedges or fencing.
❖ Avoid creating dead-end or hidden areas in shipping and receiving locations.
❖ Businesses should partner and work together to promote shopper and business safety, and create an environment that projects the appearance of safety.

❖ Morning mall-walkers can provide additional surveillance prior to opening.

TERRITORIAL REINFORCEMENT

❖ Identify individual businesses by wall signs for those parking in the rear.
❖ Mark parking locations to establish parking boundaries.
❖ Define property boundaries with landscaping, hedges, low fences, and gates.
❖ Use signage to define the behaviors desired within specific areas.
❖ Post perimeter signage at all entrances at a minimum of 100-foot intervals.
❖ Define and construct separate areas for private and public use.
❖ Install protective covering above doors and windows such as awnings and canopies.
❖ Divide parking lots into smaller individual spaces with landscaping and decorative signage.
❖ Enclave parking relative to entrances to businesses.
❖ Keep on hand available portable barriers.

MAINTENANCE

❖ Use appropriate landscaping to generate visual appeal.
❖ Keep buildings and all thoroughfares free of debris, and conduct routine repairs.
❖ Keep parking areas free of debris and possible graffiti.
❖ Keep surfaces in good repair.
❖ Conduct periodic inspections of unoccupied businesses and fill display windows with merchandise to avoid the appearance of abandonment.
❖ Keep all roadways unobstructed, and keep greenery well groomed, which will provide continual surveillance to the entire site.
❖ Maintain and monitor shelters at all bus drop-off locations to screen out outsiders.

❖ Keep dumpsters empty and visible from hidden solid walls.
❖ Keep fire escapes and emergency exits clear of obstructions.
❖ Keep exterior lighting adequate, operational, and maintained.
❖ Prohibit auto repairs, abandoned vehicles, oil spills, and other debris on the grounds.

Security cameras in mall parking area

Bus stop shelters provide safety with maintained landscaping using CPTED concepts

OFFICE STRUCTURES

The reality of living in a post 911 world has created a society increasingly concerned about the safety and well-being of its citizens, particularly those working and conducting business in large office buildings that tend to be a popular target for terrorists. Accordingly, as office buildings become mega in size and occupancy, safety and security becomes extremely important. These types of environments must provide an atmosphere of safety and trust, which will add to the overall spirit of cooperation if a disaster should occur. Conditions such as the requirement to present photo identification prior to entering the workplace, covering mail slots with metal grills, and securing garages and loading areas with steel anti-ram barricades, can make a huge difference in keeping employees and visitors safe.

<u>NATURAL ACCESS CONTROL</u>

- ❖ Locate parking areas and break-locations where there is likely to be adequate surveillance by employees and/or visitors.
- ❖ Clearly define public entrances from employee entrances with architectural features, proper lighting and landscaping, paving, and proper signage.
- ❖ Reduce the number of public access points to be visually monitored by employees, patrons, passersby, and passing traffic.
- ❖ Provide both front and rear vehicle access.
- ❖ Construct barriers or signage at locations of the buildings that are not intended for the public.
- ❖ Plainly mark public thoroughfares and regulate non-employee access to private areas.
- ❖ To allow viewing from outside the offices, position work-desks in locations that are strategic to natural surveillance.
- ❖ Prevent easy access to locations utilized by emergency service personnel (roof or fire escape) from ground level.

NATURAL SURVEILLANCE

- ❖ Remove large signs and other obstruction that can interfere with fully observing the facility.
- ❖ Design rear windows of the facility to face the parking areas, and interior windows and doors, to provide visibility into hallways.
- ❖ Design parking locations to be visible from interior windows.
- ❖ Install and apply effective lighting in all areas including hallways and exterior doors.
- ❖ Recommend that businesses establish "safe shelters" for people who feel unsafe while on the street.
- ❖ Interior displays should not obstruct visibility from the outside.
- ❖ Initiate a "Business Watch" program for additional "eyes and ears" on the street.
- ❖ Deliveries should only be accepted through a front entrance and acknowledged by a receptionist or responsible party.
- ❖ Coordinate hours of operations with neighboring businesses to avoid isolation of a single facility.
- ❖ Design public restrooms to be observable from the reception area.
- ❖ Have the entrance and exit under visual surveillance and electronically monitored.
- ❖ Concession machines should not be placed in such a way as to obstruct sight lines.
- ❖ If public phones are available, use call-out phones only.
- ❖ Avoid situations where only one employee is present.
- ❖ Design windows and exterior doors so that they are visible from the street and neighboring business places.
- ❖ Do not obstruct window view.
- ❖ Keep dumpsters discernible using care to avoid creating blind spots or hiding places, or simply position them in secured and/ or protective structures.
- ❖ Keep bushes and shrubbery under three feet in height so as not to obstruct visibility.
- ❖ Prune tree branches to at least six feet from the ground up.

Planters can serve as natural surveillance and access control. In addition, they prevent vehicles from getting too close to building fronts

TERRITORIAL REINFORCEMENT

❖ Mark parking locations to establish parking lanes and boundaries.
❖ Define property boundaries with landscaping, hedges, and low fences.
❖ If installed, position fences to maintain visibility from the street.
❖ Use signage to define the behaviors desired within specific areas.

- ❖ Post perimeter signage at all entrances at a minimum of 100-foot intervals.
- ❖ Define and construct separate areas for private and public use.
- ❖ Install protective covering above doors and windows such as awnings and canopies.
- ❖ Separate exterior private areas from public areas.

MAINTENANCE

- ❖ Use appropriate landscaping to generate visual appeal.
- ❖ Keep all roadways unobstructed, and keep greenery well groomed, which will provide continual surveillance to the entire site.
- ❖ Keep buildings and all thoroughfares free of debris, and conduct routine inspections for repairs.
- ❖ Keep parking areas free of debris and possible graffiti.
- ❖ Keep parking lot surfaces in good repair.
- ❖ Keep dumpsters empty and visible from hidden solid walls.
- ❖ Keep fire escapes and emergency exits clear of obstructions.
- ❖ Keep exterior lighting adequate, operational, and maintained.
- ❖ Prohibit auto repairs, abandoned vehicles, oil spills, and other debris on the grounds.

INDUSTRIAL STRUCTURES

Given today's climate, most industrial sites are just as concerned with safety issues as brick and mortar businesses. In fact, the nature of work done at industrial locations can often be more hazardous than the average workplace. However, issues of safety regarding crime are often given little consideration. After dark or during times where there is no work scheduled, industrial sites are usually poorly illuminated, seldom under any type of surveillance, and virtually deserted, making them potentially quite dangerous. Consequently, it is not only important to keep employees, vendors, and other visitors safe, but designers and security professionals should be informed about safety issues and make sure they understand how to address specific situations. Therefore the following CPTED strategies if implemented can reduce problems and issues:

NATURAL ACCESS CONTROL

- ❖ Limit building entrance points and monitor them.
- ❖ Locate parking areas, bus stops, and events closer to areas of increased activity.
- ❖ Provide both front and rear vehicle access.
- ❖ Provide rear access for employees and visitors to the interior of the building when rear parking is provided.
- ❖ Provide public telephones with dial-free connections to emergency service personnel.
- ❖ Prevent easy access to locations utilized by emergency service personnel (roof or fire escape) from ground level.
- ❖ Provide benches and other seating equipment to encourage pedestrian flow in specific areas.
- ❖ Construct barriers at locations of buildings that are not intended for the public.
- ❖ Plainly mark public thoroughfares and regulate non-employee access to private areas.
- ❖ Utilize signage to direct visitors to specific locations within the facility.

- Avoid designing dead-end streets, so as not to restrict surveillance opportunities from passersby and police patrols.
- Install entrance controls such as fences, gates, or security personnel, to employee parking locations.
- Assign parking locations according to preferred working shifts and to spaces that are closer to the building.
- Have separate docks for shipping and receiving, which are electronically monitored.
- Design freight yards for vehicular access by security patrols, and/or electronic monitoring.
- Avoid placing dumpsters near buildings and stacked items near loading docks that can be used to gain access to roofs.
- Use a separate entrance for small deliveries that is well marked and monitored.
- Place employee entrance, workstations, and lockers close to employee parking.
- Design nighttime parking locations that are segregated from service areas, which curtail the opportunity for pilferage.
- Restrict internal and external accesses between separate locations by distance.
- Provide access to front and rear locations of the facility to assist with patrolling the perimeter.

NATURAL SURVEILLANCE

- Remove large signs and other obstruction that can interfere with fully observing the facility.
- Design the rear windows of the facility to face the parking areas.
- Install adequate lighting at front and rear perimeters.
- Recommend businesses to establish "safe shelters" for people who feel endangered while on the street.
- Interior displays should not obstruct visibility from the outside.
- Initiate a "Business Watch" program for additional "eyes and ears" on the street.

- ❖ Design shipping and receiving areas to avoid creating hiding locations for employees, patrons, delivery personnel, and items they can steal.
- ❖ Coordinate hours of operations with neighboring businesses to avoid isolation of a single facility.
- ❖ Design public restrooms to be observable from the front entrance and/or reception area.
- ❖ Position the reception area to allow a clear view of the entire parking area.
- ❖ Have all entrances, exists, and checkouts under visual surveillance and electronically monitored.
- ❖ Concession machines and pay telephones should be in an unobstructed view of the employees.
- ❖ If public phones are available, use call-out phones only.
- ❖ Fully illuminate interior building spaces.
- ❖ Avoid situations where only one employee is present at any hour.
- ❖ Define and illuminate all entrances to be visible by passersby and police patrol units.
- ❖ Design parking locations to be visible by passersby, police patrol units, parking attendants, service personnel, and employees.
- ❖ Provide parking attendants with means to maximize visibility of the property, which should instill a sense of security.
- ❖ Utilize walls only in extreme cases, and ensure that they are the recommended height to prevent breaching.
- ❖ When designing storage yards, loading docks, and other construction, avoid creating hiding locations for possible aggressors.

TERRITORIAL REINFORCEMENT

- ❖ Industrial businesses should be identified by wall signs for those parking in the rear.
- ❖ Position parking locations to be clearly visible from interior or exterior of the building, with lanes properly marked to establish parking boundaries.

❖ Define property boundaries with landscaping, hedges, low fences, and gates.
❖ Define building boundaries with easements, signage, and graphics.
❖ Use signage to define the behaviors desired within specific areas.
❖ Post perimeter signage at all entrances at a minimum of 100-foot intervals.
❖ Define and construct separate areas for private and public use.
❖ Install protective covering above doors and windows such as awnings and canopies.
❖ Clearly define the entrance or gateway with plant features, fences, signage, and proper barriers.
❖ Restrict deliveries to daytime operating hours only.
❖ Clearly define vehicle entrances with varying paving materials and proper signage.
❖ Segregate employee and visitor parking from shipping and receiving areas.
❖ Establish anti-loitering rules.

<u>MAINTENANCE</u>

❖ Keep the building, fencing, landscaping, paths, and walkways, clean, trimmed and in good repair.
❖ Keep parking areas free of litter and trash, and the surface in good repair.
❖ Maintain signage, displays, and building evacuation instructions in good condition.
❖ Keep greenery groomed, trimmed and kept to a minimum height near windows, gates, garages, and access roads.
❖ Keep dumpsters empty and visible from hidden solid walls.
❖ Keep fire escapes and emergency exits clear of obstructions.
❖ Keep exterior lighting adequate, operational, and maintained.
❖ Prohibit auto repairs, abandoned vehicles, oil spills, and other debris on the grounds.
❖ Keep the immediate area clean and free of trash and debris.
❖ Keep garbage removal current.

Industrial building parking

Instructional signs are territorial re-enforcements

PARKING FACILITIES

Parking facilities impose environmental costs (trash, litter, abandoned vehicles), and contradict development objectives for establishing safe and secure communities. In both urban and suburban environments, parking facilities can be problematic because of poor design and maintenance, which creates blind spots and hiding places for would-be criminals and they isolate users. By properly using CPTED principles, improving the safety of these structures can be accomplished without tremendous cost. Utilization of recommended lighting intensity and other features listed below, provide parking garages and similar structures a higher level of safety.

NATURAL ACCESS CONTROL

❖ Even though physical barriers are less offensive to users, parking attendants, and/or CCTV equipment with sound monitors, can serve as a reinforcement function.

❖ Avoid ground level garage structures that can create a fortress effect on the user.

❖ Position the user entrance to the structure adjacent to the vehicle entrance.

❖ Design stairwells to be visible from ground level without the use of solid walls.

❖ Construct elevators close to main entrances that serve the lobby and floors above and below.

❖ When elevator doors open, the interior should be clearly visible.

❖ Allow no unmonitored access to adjacent buildings without direct visual contact.

❖ Elevators should not be equipped with "permanent stop buttons."

❖ Use secure closing devices.

NATURAL SURVEILLANCE

❖ Use see-through materials when constructing all elevators, including the cars wall.
❖ Install mirrors on all sides of the elevator walls, or aluminum convex mirrors at angles.
❖ Design stairwells with enclosed glass.
❖ Construct solid barrier walls with stretched cable railings for maximum visibility.
❖ Fully illuminate all parking areas and driving lanes with proper lighting. Metal Halide lamps provide the best color rendition for nighttime viewing.
❖ Design round columns if possible to avoid hiding places.
❖ Ground spaces should be dedicated to pedestrian oriented activities.
❖ Establish operating hours to reflect those of nearby businesses.

TERRITORIAL REINFORCEMENT

❖ Differentiate between public and private spaces.
❖ Segregate visitor parking from employee parking.
❖ Identify the intended use by proper signage.
❖ Use signage to post a "hot line" for reporting suspicious behavior and/or maintenance issues.
❖ Use symbols, numbers or color codes, to assist the user in locating their vehicles.

MAINTENANCE

❖ Keep all surfaces clean and coated with light-color to reflect light. If underground, use white paint.
❖ Use vandal proof screens or covers on light fixtures.
❖ Keep landscaping properly trimmed, and all lighting and surveillance equipment in good working condition.
❖ Regularly check for and remove graffiti.

❖ Reflective paint or materials should be used in all areas to increase feelings of safety.

❖ Keep facility clear of abandoned vehicles, trash, and debris.

Openings allow viewing of parking areas

PARKS, VENUES AND OPEN AREAS

As we enter the 21st century, the population remains on the rise and the development of open spaces, parks, and public recreational facilities is following the growth trend. Hence, there are a number of challenges regarding personal safety that should command the immediate attention of architects, developers, law enforcement, and security personnel. As it has already been said many times in this book and bears repeating; since it is nearly impossible to provide personal security to everyone who uses these spaces, CPTED principles should be considered during the designing, remodeling or assessing stages of any new project.

Open and highly visible play area

NATURAL ACCESS CONTROL

❖ Post signage at all park entryways at a minimum of 100 foot intervals, but legible from not less than 50 feet.
❖ Use language common to the area of concern.

- ❖ Provide clear unobstructed entryways to park facilities, with proper lighting for nighttime usage.
- ❖ If the park closes at night, use proper signage that indicates facility usage during daytime only, to control access.
- ❖ Construct a clear distance between the trails and wood-lines to provide adequate site-lines and distances from potential violators.
- ❖ Define clear separation between trails and private property, which would provide a quick departure in emergencies.
- ❖ Design a clear and observable alternate path to all trails, to provide safer mobility to its users.

NATURAL SURVEILLANCE

- ❖ Cluster activities to avoid conflict and to increase observation by participants.
- ❖ Provide a roadway through the park to facilitate police or security patrols.
- ❖ Locate picnic areas, activity centers and other facilities that are accessible at night, near thoroughfares that are observable by patrol units and other park users.
- ❖ Locate recreation areas and public restrooms near staffed locations to provide easy observation of these areas.
- ❖ Young children and tot areas should not be located near streets, roadways, trails or secluded areas. Tot areas should be fenced-in using tubular steel material to increase safety and observation.
- ❖ Position bike trails and pathways near areas that encompass park activities or at locations near commercial or residential personnel, which can serve as additional eyes and ears against potential violators.
- ❖ Some parks cannot be observable or made safe during night hours and should therefore be closed during nighttime.
- ❖ If possible, provide proper or upscale lighting to areas that can be used safely during nighttime hours.
- ❖ Trim or remove major foliage obstructions.

TERRITORIAL REINFORCEMENT

❖ Provide children's play areas to attract families to park facilities, which will define appropriate uses.

❖ Create separate activity areas designed for different users.

❖ Define areas with plant/foliage and/or physical barriers.

❖ Clearly define pathways between parking locations and other facilities.

❖ Provide mapping to express direction and a sense of location for normal users. The maps should identify trails by names, distances to various other facilities in the park, emergency contact equipment, and the uniqueness of the trails (descriptions).

❖ Erect park rules and guidelines at all access and gathering locations in the park. The rules should define acceptable uses and discourage unacceptable uses of the space.

❖ Erect directional signage to trails, play areas and other areas of public activity, and use mile markers to guide users. Define trails according to its uses (hiking, jogging, walking, biking, etc.).

MAINTENANCE

❖ Trim greenery to keep paths clear and to eliminate hiding areas and other areas of concealment.

❖ Use adequate trash receptacles at locations where people assemble with durable vandal resistant material.

❖ Remove graffiti and trash promptly when needed.

❖ Provide park benches with seat-dividers to discourage long-term usage such as loitering or sleeping.

❖ If fixtures are present, provide vandal proof lighting for normal users.

Park bench with dividers

Signage define uses

4 TARGET HARDENING APPROACH

Target hardening is a term predominantly used by police officers and security professionals, referring to strengthening the security of structures in order to reduce or minimize the risk or threat of attack. Physical barriers such as locks, bolts, and anti-fraud devices, although traditional approaches, can be of great assistance in preventing crime, but at the same time, can create an impression that crime is prevalent in the area. Therefore by employing CPTED principles, maximum security can be utilized, while lessening the visual impact on the neighborhood or business district.

RESIDENTIAL DISTRICT

❖ Improve locking devices by installing double-cylinder deadbolt locks to interior doors that are connected to exterior facilities.

❖ If single-cylinder deadbolts locks are installed, use a minimum one inch throw on exit doors, with proper screws at the base of the "strike" plates.

❖ The "strike" is the metal plate that attaches to the doorjamb and receives the bolt. This should be installed using three-inch screws. Using long screws secures the strike to the doorframe, not just the jamb. In addition, the lock should also have a reinforced strike plate with offset screw holes. The offset holes ensure that the screws are not driven into the same grain of wood. When someone is trying to kick in a door, the jamb will normally give way before the deadbolt; but the extra long screws and reinforced plate will stand up to serious impact.

❖ The locks should be located at least 40 inches from adjacent windows or glass openings.

❖ The weakest area in all windows is generally the glass, therefore to discourage penetration, polycarbonate (plastic material), and a special plastic laminate (sandwiched between two pieces of glass) could be used, which are highly resistant to impact.

❖ Sliding or rolling glass doors (single or double) may be used on tracks or rollers. Sliding glass doors should have a wooden rod in the track so it cannot be opened and locking pins in the overhead frame so it cannot be lifted out. Doors should also be protected to prevent breaching at the undercarriage.

❖ Install door viewers (peepholes) at least 180° and 1/2" Bore on doors 1 3/8" to 2" thick.

❖ Identify personal property with indelible markings.

❖ Change codes to alarms, garage door openers, and any combination-locking unit, at least twice a year.

❖ Remove possible crime targets such as portable yard equipment.

❖ Trim trees that may enable access to upper level rooms.

INSTITUTIONAL ESTABLISHMENTS

❖ Limit access to all entrances and position all work-areas to permit viewing from the entrances.

❖ Reduce the reward of crime by removing crime magnets or making them less valuable to the offender.

❖ Keep expensive computer and office equipment securely locked.

❖ Install magnetic sensors in library books and materials.

❖ Initiate a no-cash policy, keep valuable equipment in secure areas during closing hours, and substitute sturdier equipment for equipment that can be vandalized.

❖ Identify property with permanent markings to establish ownership, preventing the resale of the property.

❖ Remove car radios in maintenance vehicles.

❖ Use tokens for laundry, vending machines, and phone-cards for public telephones.

- ❖ Make phone listings gender-neutral to eliminate sexual harassment.
- ❖ Cover graffiti-prone areas with thorny greenery.
- ❖ Use sign-in for guests, and identification information for employees.
- ❖ In extreme cases, use CCTV video cameras and monitors, security personnel, and security hardware, as deterrents for unwanted activities.
- ❖ Use baffle restroom entrances (an opening without actual doors)
- ❖ In extreme or special situations, use metal detectors or trained dogs.
- ❖ Make all exterior signage (gate, parking, etc.) out of wooden material. Metal signs encourage "sign-shooting" due to the sound that is produced when struck.
- ❖ Contact local law enforcement to request special attention with police patrols.

Building has hardened security features

PUBLIC HOUSING

- ❖ Install high quality security locks.
- ❖ Install an intercom to screen visitors.
- ❖ Install peepholes (wide view) on front and rear doors.
- ❖ Design lighting systems with emergency backup power units.
- ❖ Use an entry control package with Closed Circuit Television (CCTV), such as the "pan-tilt-zoom" system at the security desk, if possible.
- ❖ Initiate a visitor control/screening process.
- ❖ Use an intrusion detection system with central monitoring.
- ❖ Install a duress alarm with central monitoring.
- ❖ Establish a roving guard patrol on site.
- ❖ Initiate a controlled utility access location for service personnel.
- ❖ Establish an annual employee security-training program.
- ❖ Use roller shutters, window grills, bars, and mesh.

COMMERCIAL ESTABLISHMENTS

- ❖ Install door viewers (peepholes) at least 180º and 1/2" Bore on doors 1 3/8" to 2" thick, with secure frames.
- ❖ Use "drop safes" during transactions to limit the availability of cash to potential offenders.
- ❖ Place height markers on exit doors to assist potential witnesses with providing assistance in the description of possible assailants.
- ❖ Use door detectors to alert employees when persons enter the establishment.
- ❖ Use silent and personal alarms to notify police or management in the event of a problem.
- ❖ When making bank deposits after hours, employees should proceed in pairs.
- ❖ Install video cameras with monitors, but store the recording devices in inconspicuous locations. Some security professionals recommend using decoy devices to mislead possible offenders.

❖ Adopt proper emergency procedures for employees to use in case of a robbery or security breach.
❖ Lock doors used for deliveries and garbage disposal when not is use.
❖ Provide employees with adequate safety and security training.

Commercial building with hardened security features

MALLS/SHOPPING CENTERS

❖ Install acoustically monitored shopper traffic surveillance and security cameras.
❖ Install high-intensity lighting in parking lots to provide detailed illumination.
❖ Install cop-towers and/or establish mini-patrol units.

Cop-tower

Mini-patrols

OFFICE STRUCTURES

- ❖ Keep all doors secured and do not block emergency exits.
- ❖ Empty all trash during daylight hours.
- ❖ Implement safety procedures for employees under emergency conditions.
- ❖ Have police and/or security personnel vary their patrol schedule and routes.
- ❖ Take measures to avoid unmonitored exit doors from being propped open.

INDUSTRIAL STRUCTURES

- ❖ Increase intensity of lighting around the perimeter of the property.
- ❖ Make sure all padlocking devices are fully secured, and not left in an open position (thieves can replace padlocks with their own).
- ❖ Do not leave key-controlled devices in open position, thieves can have keys made or replaced with similar locks with their own keys.
- ❖ Periodically change all locks and/or combinations, and limit the number of keys available.
- ❖ Use interchangeable or removable core locks.

❖ In locking systems, do not utilize a single control or grand master scheme (codes), to prevent from totally compromising the system in case of physical loss.

PARKING FACILITIES

❖ Install zoned and clearly recognized parking, with insignia in bright colored paints and large numbers to identify levels that reflect light.

❖ Intensify lighting over the driving lanes to provide illumination of people outside of the vehicle.

❖ Install panic alarms or emergency phone-stations (with flashing lights) on each floor to provide added safety features.

❖ Allow parking attendants to patrol in mini-vehicles that emit discernible flashing caution lights.

PARKS, VENUES AND OPEN AREAS

❖ Provide emergency communication systems with flashing lights.

❖ Provide high-intensity lighting for nighttime illumination.

❖ Define and enforce operation hours.

❖ Contact local law enforcement to request special attention with patrol units during all shifts.

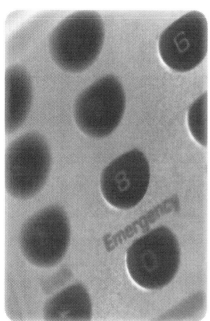

Emergency communication for parking garage

Emergency communication for trails & walkways

5 LIGHTING TECHNIQUES

PROTECTIVE LIGHTING

Adequate lighting is essential to any protection of assets plan. Lighting is used for protection, illumination, and sometimes as a barrier. Abnormal users prefer to act under the cover of darkness, and well-lit areas certainly discourage illegal or criminal acts. Lighting used strictly for illumination, functions as a safety precaution for docks and bridges and as a marker to delineate lanes and drops. In addition, lighting can be used as a barrier to restrict access to controlled areas. All of the aforementioned uses of lighting are strategies within the CPTED model.

Lighting has multiple functions, which include but are not limited to the following:

- ❖ Encourage routine activity.
- ❖ Causes pedestrians, as well as other vehicles to be more visible to motorists, enhances the ability to observe surroundings, as well as objects that should be avoided.
- ❖ Aids witnesses in describing suspects and identifying perpetrators.
- ❖ Operates as a physical deterrent through the glare method (light glares into the eyes of a potential intruder).
- ❖ To be a psychological deterrent by leading attackers to believe that they will be discovered, and observed making an attack or penetration attempt.

❖ Support and enhance CCTV operation.
❖ Discourage illegal activities by criminals who wish to go undetected.

To understand the language of lighting standards, security professionals and practitioners must be familiar with the following lighting terminology:

❖ Lumen – a measure of light at its source and amount of light output.
❖ Foot-candle – a measure of light striking the surface 1 square foot in an area which one unit of light (lumen) is uniformly distributed.
❖ Lux – a measure of illumination that is 1/10th of a foot-candle.
❖ Luminaries – the complete light fixture (light source and ballast).

Sources of light will include:

❖ Incandescent – Produces light by running electric current through a filament wire. Some of the advantages of this type of lighting are – instant warm-up and restart, excellent color rendition, can be dimmable, very compact, works well with motion sensors, and has good to excellent optical control. Some of the disadvantages are – inefficiency (emits 10-38 lumens per watt), has short lamp life (only 500 hours), and has a high heat output.
❖ Florescent – Low-pressure mercury discharge in which a phosphor coating transforms ultraviolet energy into light. Some of the advantages of this type of lighting are – has long lamp life (12,000 – 20,000 hours), emits 67-83 lumens per watt, efficient operation, good color rendition, instant warm-up and restart, and has moderate initial cost. Some of the disadvantages are – fair optical control, extended in size, and can be affected by cold air and temperature.

❖ Mercury Vapor – High-intensity discharge producing light by mercury vapor. Some of the advantages are – emits bluish white light, has long life (16,000 – 24,000 hours), has fair to good color rendition, and good optical control. Some of the disadvantages are – inefficiency (emits 45-63 lumens per watt), has high initial cost, light output decreases rapidly over the life of the source, warm-up takes 5-8 minutes, and restart takes 10-20 minutes.

❖ Metal Halide – Advantages: emits sparkling white light, has long lamp life (6,000 – 20,000 hours), very compact, excellent color rendition, and good optical control and restart. Disadvantages: inefficiency (emits 80-100 lumens per watt), has high cost, takes 5-8 minutes to warm-up, and 10-20 minutes to restart.

❖ High Pressure Sodium – Advantages: emits pink or golden light, has long life (16,000 – 24,000 hours), emits 80-140 lumens per watt, very compact, fair to good color rendition, good – fair optical control, and good restart. Disadvantages: takes 2-5 minutes to warm-up, and has high cost.

❖ Low Pressure Sodium – Advantages – emits yellow light, very efficient (18,000 – 20,000 hours), emits 139-183 lumens per watt and can restart from 0-8 minutes. Disadvantages: poor color rendition, fair optical control, extended in size, high cost, takes 5-8 minutes to warm-up.

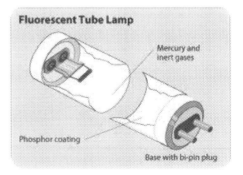

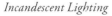

Incandescent Lighting   *Fluorescent Lighting*

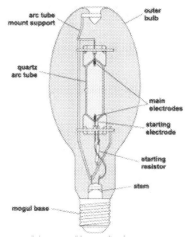

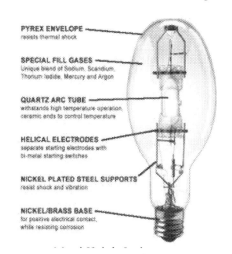

Mercury Vapor Lighting   *Metal Halide Lighting*

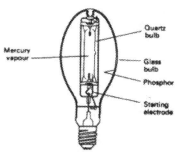

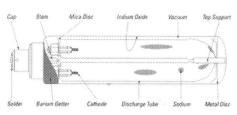

High pressure sodium lighting   *Low-pressure sodium lighting*

Even though there is no current U.S. national standard for protective or security lighting systems, protection professionals recommend a minimum of 2.0-foot candles of maintained lighting level. However, the Illumination Engineering Society (IES, the lighting authority publisher of lighting design and illuminations standards) has determined that the below listed lighting levels specified are the minimum average levels acceptable.

Location	Lighting Level
High Risk Activity: ATM, Cluster Mail Boxes, Pay Phones, Gated Community Entries, Pedestrian Tunnels and Covered Pedestrian Walkways (breezeways), Bus/ Transit Shelters, All exterior entrances	4-5 foot candles
Medium High Risk Activity: Convenience Stores, Covered Parking (carports), Fast Food, Pharmacies, Pool Halls, Loading Docks/Areas, Grocery Stores (24 hour, immediate parking area), Establishments Licensed for the Sale of Liquor, Parking Structures (10 FC daytime)	3-4 foot candles
Medium Low Risk Activity: Multi-Housing, Health Care, Industrial (night use), Preschools, Worship, Hospital, General Retail, Dental, Warehouse (night use), Educational, Storage, General Office (night use), Grocery Stores (non 24 hours)	1-2 foot candles
Low Risk Activity: Warehouse (day use), Office (day use only), Greenbelt, Car Dealers (after hours), Parks, Industrial (day use), Mini-storage, Retention Areas, Walkways in Apartment Complexes	0.50-1 foot candles

6 LANDSCAPING TECHNIQUES

Landscaping can either add to or take away from the aesthetics of a property. Lush and well-maintained trees, shrubbery and plants, tell others that the property has active guardians and certain behaviors are not tolerated. Conversely, overgrown or poorly maintained landscaping can be a sure sign of abandoned property or that which the dwellers have no vested interest. The latter are a haven for criminals, and those desiring to commit illegal, dishonest, and/or immoral acts. Therefore, adopting CPTED strategies with regard to landscaping, can greatly enhance the safety of normal users.

CPTED landscaping techniques can be used to establish ownership or define borders, which will discourage abnormal users from congregating. Below are some guidelines regarding the proper maintenance of trees, shrubs and other greenery:

❖ Use low-growing ground cover only.
❖ Shrubs and trees should not interfere with security lighting or other points of surveillance from streets, parks, open spaces or buildings.
❖ Trim, relocate or remove trees, bushes, hedges, fences, etc., when needed.
❖ Hedges and bushes should not be greater than three feet high.
❖ The lowest tree branch should be six feet or more above the ground.
❖ Trim trees away from lighting systems.
❖ When placing greenery next to or between buildings and along paths and sidewalks, shrubs, bushes, hedges, and branches

should be trimmed to provide two to six feet of clearance space.

❖ If graffiti is an issue in the area, use thorny greenery, planters or ivy for landscape as a natural barrier to deter unwanted access.

❖ To deter graffiti specifically, use vines and/or planted wall coverings.

❖ If graffiti is present, eliminate the first graffiti immediately, which should eliminate the responses.

❖ Remove inducements for crime by avoiding blank spaces on walls, which may be inviting to graffiti vandals.

FENCING

Much like lighting, fencing can be a valuable component in an integrated protection scheme. Of the various fence types utilized with lighting systems, the most popular by far is chain link fencing. Due to its quick installation, durability and cheap cost, it can be effective against vehicles, animals, and persons, if properly installed. Even though chain link fencing can be easily crossed without breaching aids such as blankets, bolt and wire cutters, standard chain link fencing will serve as a deterrent to some vehicles, casual intruders, animals, or those seeking targets of opportunity.

CPTED strategies espouse the use of chain link fencing for almost any application where it is necessary that a boundary be defined or where a barrier is needed. However, proper installation is very important, and using the following guidelines will ensure a successful outcome:

❖ Avoid solid fencing, which increases the need for security personnel.

❖ Provide fencing that does not create blind spots or hiding places for wrongdoers.

❖ Provide attractive and durable fencing to meet the threat.

❖ Use fence lighting in the landscaping to enhance visibility and security.

❖ When constructing "privacy fences", raise the fencing four to six inches above ground to allow the exposure of anyone behind the fence.

❖ When constructing chain link or wrought iron fencing, mesh openings should not be more than two-inch-by-two-inch squares for chain link and four inches for wrought iron.

❖ Construct fencing at minimum height of seven feet, not including the top guard.

❖ Use nine-gauge or higher mesh.

❖ Move or remove trees, poles or other objects that can be used to scale the fence.

❖ Protect any opening of 96 square inches or greater.

❖ Protect any opening greater than six inches in the smallest dimension.

❖ Protect any opening that is located within 18 feet from the ground, ledge or roof.

❖ Perimeter fencing should be illuminated five feet on either side.

Low-level landscaping design

Fencing as landscaping aesthetics

7 ACCESS CONTROL TECHNIQUES

Access control systems are implemented to protect persons, materials, or information against any type of harm which could include; injury to people or damage to material, and to permit or deny entry to any given area or item(s). In short, the overall purpose for access control is to increase the effort needed to commit a crime. There are various techniques to employ when initiating efforts to deny or grant access to a given location, and ranges from simple locking devices to state-of-the-art equipment. The following describes some of the solutions that are beneficial and currently available to assist in reducing criminal activity:

❖ Installing barriers to prevent unwanted users from entering restricted areas.
❖ Improving locking devices, interior and exterior sensors.
❖ Using electrical and electronic touch-pads.
❖ Using guards, card reader systems (smart cards, magnetic stripes barcodes), and biometric readers.
❖ Using resident photo identifications and CCTV systems.
❖ Installing entry phones, visitor check-in booths and guard booths.

SITUATIONAL PREVENTION

Situational crime prevention is based on a theory of crime prevention developed by Ronald V. Clarke in his book published in 1992. His theory underscores a targeted means of reducing crime with four objectives in mind: 1) increasing the effort needed to commit the crime; 2) increasing the risks associated with the crime; 3) reducing the rewards of crime; and 4) removing excuses or creating embarrassment. These objectives work in conjunction with ***access control*** to increase the effort needed to commit a crime by:

- ❖ Providing criminal offenders alternate and legal venues for their activities.
- ❖ Controlling the behavior of persons in volatile situations, such as separating spectators after sports activities.
- ❖ Combating drug activity by targeting the demand side (purchasers) as opposed to the supply side (sellers).
- ❖ Broadcast enforcement results that send the message that perpetrators will be prosecuted to the full extent of the law.
- ❖ Identify and engage in countering the influx of crowds attracted by casinos, theatres, and major sports events.
- ❖ Remove or camouflage accessories that can aid in committing crimes.
- ❖ Increase enforcement efforts against prostitution, the sale of drug paraphernalia, and illegal alcohol.
- ❖ Target abandoned and vacant housing that are precursors for drug activity.
- ❖ Remove abandoned shopping carts, vehicles, and other crime magnets.
- ❖ Request the enforcement of curfew and trespassing laws.

8 CLOSED CIRCUIT TELEVISION (CCTV) SPECIFICATIONS

CCTV coverage can be limited in scope, but can still provide adequate security coverage when properly installed. When placed at main entrances, exit control points, fencing, and other locations, CCTV can be used for continuous monitoring and can be connected to video recorders for future playback. Electronic security with digitization greatly enhances CCTV, and a vast amount of recorded information can be stored electronically on compact disks.

For security professionals, it is extremely important to discuss the roles of electronic security. The components consist of: 1) Deterrence; 2) Detection; 3) Delaying; 4) Assessment and 5) Response.

❖ Deterrence – to discourage easy access and to reinforce boundaries with the aid of barriers, walls, fences, gates, and locking devices.
❖ Detection – to provide early warning of unauthorized entry with the aid of intrusion detection sensors.
❖ Delaying – to impede easy access to valued assets with the aid of barriers, fences, delay devices, and audiovisual alerts.
❖ Assessment – to delay the intruder to assess the details of his/ her actions with the aid of visual identification, lighting systems, audio, and CCTV central stations.
❖ Response – to respond quickly and take the appropriate action with the assistance of security and police personnel, communication systems, and emergency medical personnel.

CCTV capability strengthens safety and the effectiveness and efficiency of security in three important methods: 1) Advances in CCTV technology offer a host of opportunities for integration of the systems in public and private institutions. 2) CCTV operates as an extension of the human eyes and ears in a wide variety of security settings. With its ability to monitor several locations simultaneously, CCTV can be very cost effective as well. 3) CCTV systems can provide a permanent record of a recorded event or incident, which can be made available to law enforcement if necessary.

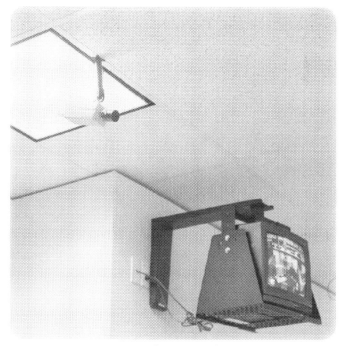

Access control system with CCTV

COMPLETING THE SECURITY SURVEY/ ASSESSMENT REPORT

The security survey/assessment is prepared by security professionals to anticipate, identify, and assess crime and/or security vulnerabilities and risks; then subsequently provide recommendations to remove or minimize harm from potential threats. The following outline can be used to complete an accurate and concise report:

GENERAL INFORMATION

❖ **Introduction/Executive Summary** – describes the physical layout of the facility (type of construction and design materials), location, date the survey was performed and by whom, crime rates in the area, weather susceptibility and social conditions.

❖ **Assessment Planning** – research methods, continuous risk assessment, contingency plans, and business operations continuity.

❖ **Physical Security** – Facility Perimeter (border definition), which includes fencing, landscaping, designated parking areas, signage and shipping & receiving area monitoring; Building Layout, which includes entrances and emergency exits, doors, stairwells, locks, windows, roof, and lighting system; Access Controls, which includes intrusion detectors (CCTV with recorders), key control, visitor/guest entrance monitoring, employee identification, specialty room restrictions – mailroom, telecommunications, utility, executive suites/offices, safe/vault, and asset protection.

❖ **Threats/Risk Vulnerabilities** – Natural Access Control, Natural Surveillance, Territorial Reinforcement and Maintenance.

❖ **Findings** – observed vulnerable and risk factors.

❖ **Recommendations** – implement CPTED strategies to decrease and/or eliminate the vulnerabilities and risk factors by removing, repairing, replacing, installing or reallocating the physical space.

9 NEIGHBORHOOD WATCH STRATEGIES

NEIGHBORHOOD WATCH

Statistics support that Neighborhood Watch programs are effective in decreasing crime and the fear of crime, and increasing the quality of life for the communities in which it is practiced. Although the criminal justice system – the police, courts and prisons – are effective tools, they are primarily reactive as they deal with crime after it takes place. While there is little doubt that law enforcement can play an important role in preventing crime by making arrests, neighbors and residents are generally the first to observe suspicious activity and the first to contact authorities, thus the use of "eyes and ears" by neighbors is the most effective pro-active approach to crime prevention.

Security professionals highly recommend the following neighborhood watch programs, which can be beneficial to the community in the following ways:

- ❖ Groups of neighbors can band together to form political action committees to pressure city hall.
- ❖ Neighbors can detect the kinds of crimes that rarely get news coverage and coordinate enforcement efforts with local law enforcement.
- ❖ Implement crime awareness programs, which result in safer communities.

❖ In taking the initiative for crime prevention, neighbors not only keep criminals at bay, but also help to reduce the potential for abuse of authority by public officials.

❖ Provide neighbors with all important crime statistics to assist them in crafting counter measures.

❖ Neighbors can perform maintenance of overgrown shrubs and other greenery that might be detrimental to natural surveillance and pressure also city hall to improve street lighting, which can discourage wrongdoers from committing crimes because of the threat of detection.

❖ Receive individual home security surveys and threat assessments.

❖ Neighbors can befriend neighborhood children to prevent them from joining gangs or other subversive groups, or possibly assist/ advise a victim of domestic violence and help him/her to make decisions that would decrease the potential for the abuse to escalate into a violent tragedy.

Types of neighborhood watch programs include:

WINDOW WATCH

Window watchers are often residents who are housebound for reasons of health, advanced age, disability, a primary caregiver in the home, etc. Window watching involves keeping the neighborhood under observation by continually looking out of windows and doors, and reporting any suspicious activity to the police.

In order to accomplish this, a schedule must be set for the window watchers who follow a strict observation routine. The benefit of this watch strategy is to augment the larger Neighborhood Watch program with strategic limited objectives.

WALKING PATROLS

Many Neighborhood Watch programs assign residents to walk within a certain area to actively look for suspicious activities. The walking patrols are conducted in pairs during periods that crime is most likely to occur. Upon observing suspicious activities, walking patrols are to contact the police by dialing 911, using a cell phone that is designated only for the program. Patrol personnel are reminded that they are to serve as "eyes and ears", and are cautioned against personal intervention or confrontation.

NATIONAL WATCH

The National Night Out campaign is a widely known national watch program which involves citizens, law enforcement agencies, civic groups, businesses, neighborhood organizations, and local officials from over 15,000 communities within all 50 states, U.S. territories, Canadian cities, and military bases worldwide. In all, over 37 million people participated in National Night Out 2010 (National Association of Town Watch, 2011). National Night Out is designed to:

- ❖ Heighten crime and drug prevention awareness.
- ❖ Generate support for, and participation in, local anticrime programs.
- ❖ Strengthen neighborhood spirit and police-community partnerships.
- ❖ Send a message to criminals that neighborhoods are organized and fighting back.

BUSINESS WATCH

Business Watch programs were formed to help reduce crimes in neighborhood commercial areas such as shoplifting, fraud, burglaries, criminal mischief, and other illicit activities. The program serves to build relationships among businesses within a community by encouraging employees and residents to watch out for each other and maintain a safe shopping and working environment. The program also provides a forum for education and community solutions, and a network with local law enforcement regarding criminal activity affecting local businesses and the community at large, with the following benefits in mind:

- ❖ Creates a crime prevention partnership between targeted community businesses and local law enforcement.
- ❖ To reduce crime-related financial losses to businesses and to reduce the fear of crime from both the business owner and the customer perspective.
- ❖ To prevent computer scams and confidence schemes directed toward businesses, as well as the crimes of shoplifting and vandalism.
- ❖ To assist the local community with multiple sets of "eyes and ears", as a joint effort in curtailing criminal activities.
- ❖ To improve communication between business proprietors and local law enforcement.
- ❖ To solicit information and ideas from the public, which could increase the efficiency and effectiveness of the Program.
- ❖ To encourage business owners to fully embrace security measures in order to deter crime.
- ❖ Receive individual business security surveys and threat assessments.

FLEET WATCH

Fleet Watch is a formal community service program sponsored by area utility, business, and public agencies, to help maintain law and order. The goal of the program is to use commercial drivers as an extra set of "eyes and ears" to observe and report suspicious activities or emergencies. Fleet Watch offers a unified and visible service to all communities. The best and most cost effective crime prevention resource available to law enforcement is the community.

WORSHIP AND SCHOOL WATCHES

Churches, alternate places of worship and schools, also need extra "sets of eyes" in the neighborhood to watch for problems that might arise such as vandalism, trespassing, theft, or mechanical breakdown. These programs can also provide "eyes" to alert the police when acts of violence threaten the peace and stability of neighborhoods and other nearby facilities. Residents whose homes are situated such that they have a clear view of churches and schools are encouraged to be on the lookout for suspicious, criminal, or related acts.

Worship and School Watch programs are modeled after Neighborhood Watch programs, which heighten awareness in neighborhoods to activities that should not be occurring, and for which the observers should notify the police.

Neighborhood watch alert

SCAM/FRAUD WATCH

As the financial markets both in the U.S. and abroad face rising instability, scams and fraud are also at an all time high. Unscrupulous persons are attempting to benefit from the misfortune of others by any means necessary, but especially by scams and fraudulent actions. A scam is described as an illegal scheme to make money by trickery or deception. Many scams rely on unsuspecting persons handing over or being tricked out of information that is generally kept secret. On the other hand, fraud can be broadly defined as an intentional act of deception involving financial transactions for the purpose of personal gain. To protect people from becoming victims, it is recommended that the public become aware of the most common **scams** and **frauds**, which are described below:

- ❖ Unemployment and Jobs – promotes unemployment as a "state service", which requires the completion of an application along with a fee to process the unemployment benefits. After the fee is paid, the applicant discovers that unemployment funds are no-cost benefits provided to eligible American workers.
- ❖ Extortion – on-line caller claims the victim is delinquent in a payday loan and must repay the loan to avoid legal action. Callers purport to be representatives of U.S. government agencies, and are collecting debts for known internet check-cashing services.
- ❖ Loan Modification – the scam artist poses as a counselor and tells you he/she can negotiate a deal with your lender to modify your loan or save your home if you pay a fee first. Once the fee is paid, the counselor disappears.
- ❖ Prime Bank Note – this investment scheme offers high yields in a short period of time. Criminals claim to have access to "bank guarantees", which they are able to buy at a discount, and turn around and sell at a premium. By reselling the "bank guarantees", they promise victims huge returns on their investments.
- ❖ Ponzi Scheme – is an investment fraud where criminals promise high financial returns or dividends not available through ordinary investments. Instead of investing the victim's money, the con artist will pay "dividends" to initial investors using money "invested" by subsequent investors.
- ❖ Pyramid Scheme – marketing and investment frauds where victims are offered the opportunity to market a product. The real profit is not made by the sale of the product, but by the sale of a subsequent victim buying into that same opportunity to market the same product. Participants are promised return on their original investments by initiating two or more prospects

to make the same investment. The supply of potential investors eventually falls off and as a result, the pyramid collapses.

❖ <u>Redemption/Straw-Man/Bond Fraud</u> – involves criminals who claim the U.S. Government or the Treasury Department controls all bank accounts and for a fee can be accessed in order to erase debt or purchase merchandise. The con artist operating this scam usually refers to the process as "Redemption," "Straw-Man" or "Acceptance for Value."

❖ <u>Medicare</u> – scammers fake signatures or bribe corrupt doctors to sign Medicare forms certifying that equipment or services are needed. Once a signature is secured, Medicare is billed for merchandise or services.

❖ <u>Medical Equipment</u> – individuals are offered free products from equipment manufacturers, insurers are then subsequently charged for products that were not needed or may not have been received.

❖ <u>Services Not Performed</u> – providers or customers bill insurers for services never rendered, by changing the bills and submitting fake ones.

❖ <u>Rolling Lab</u> – unnecessary or fake tests provided at health clubs, shopping malls or rest homes, then billed to Medicare or insurance companies.

❖ <u>Health Insurance</u> – a provider submits a claim for payment to which they not entitled, or falsifies the documentation supporting the claim.

Recommendations to avoid Health Insurance Scams/Fraud:

❖ Maintain accurate records of all health care appointments.
❖ Provide insurance or Medicare identification only to those who have provided the actual service.
❖ Never sign blank insurance claim forms.
❖ Enquire about charges and out-of-pocket expenses from your medical provider prior to the service.
❖ Never provide absolute authorization to a medical provider to bill for services rendered.

❖ Never conduct business with telephone or door-to-door sales people who attempt to convince you that medical equipment is free of charge.
❖ Carefully review the statement explaining the insurance benefits, and contact the provider for possible questions.

Recommendations to avoid Extortion Scams/Fraud:

❖ If contacted by telephone, do not follow caller's instructions.
❖ Contact your banking institution immediately.
❖ Contact the three main credit bureaus (Equifax, Experian and TransUnion) to attach an alert to your file.
❖ Contact local law enforcement if you feel threatened.
❖ Contact the Internet Crime Complaint Center (IC3) to file a complaint.

10 ABANDONED/FORECLOSED PROPERTIES

Because of the economic crisis suffered by the subprime lending market, mortgage foreclosures have continued to climb across the country with the greatest concentration in high poverty neighborhoods (Baker, 2007). Consequently, communities are currently faced with a profusion of neglected or abandoned properties. These properties are crime magnets that attract squatters, and drug dealers who use them for criminal activity. Short of razing these properties, the following security recommendations can alleviate the problem and transform distressed neighborhoods into healthy and sustainable places to live, work, and conduct business:

❖ Partner with local law enforcement agencies to create a task force to combat the initial problem of neighborhood blight due to abandoned properties.

❖ Follow up with local law enforcement to encourage them to monitor neighbors that are known to have an abundance of foreclosures.

❖ Communicate with community leaders so they are aware of the impact of foreclosures on crime and neighborhood safety.

❖ Assist in providing information to help homeowners avoid losing their homes and minimize the impact on areas where properties have already been abandoned or foreclosed.

❖ Recommend and provide access to available foreclosure assistance and counseling programs.

❖ Step up community policing techniques to identify problem properties.

❖ Collaborate with neighborhood organizations that target revitalization programs.

❖ Identify owners of nuisance properties and specify nature of the problem.

❖ Ensure that properties are properly secured and given special attention by local law enforcement patrols.

❖ Encourage local law enforcement and city government to issue violation notices to address specific concerns.

❖ Partner with city, state, county, and federal officials, to take advantage of new resources from federal assistance and private sector initiatives.

❖ Establish collaborative relationships with developers, real estate brokers, and financial institutions, as well as nonprofit organizations.

❖ Meet with local banks to develop a strategy to assist with combating the growing problem of foreclosures.

❖ Encourage individual investors to purchase, rehab, or remodel- foreclosed property, or to resale those properties.

❖ Collaborate with major community development organizations such as Habitat for Humanity and Sprite Tabs for Habitat for assistance.

11 CRUSADE AGAINST WORKPLACE VIOLENCE

WORKPLACE VIOLENCE (WPV)

Workplace violence (WPV) is any act, which occurs in the workplace that results in threatened or actual harm to persons or property. Violence in the workplace is a topic that concerns employees and employers alike. According to the Department of Labor, Bureau of Labor Statistics (BLS), mass shootings in the workplace have recently received a great deal of coverage in the media. As evidenced by the Orlando, FL., office shootings in November 2009 and the shootings at a manufacturing plant in Albuquerque, N.M., in July 2010, workplace violence can have devastating effects on the productivity of organizations and on the quality of life of the employees. Out of 421 workplace shootings recorded in 2008 (8% of the total were fatal injuries), 99 (24%) occurred in retail trade. Workplace shootings in manufacturing were less common, with 17 shootings reported in 2008, and they account for only a small portion of nonfatal workplace injuries.

Although homicide in the workplace has always been a major concern, a more disturbing trend has surfaced. As reported by the BLS Census of Fatal Occupational Injuries (CFOI) system data for calendar year 2003, homicides were the second leading cause of death on the job for women, and 15% of the 119 workplace homicides of women in that year were attributed to a current or former husband or boyfriend. Other perpetrators consisted of employees, spouses or other companions,

Clint Kirkwood

customers, and suppliers to the businesses. Even when a death did not occur, the perpetrator's actions caused varying problems for surviving family members, which not only affected them personally, but also had an adverse effect on their communities.

Under the Federal Occupational Health and Safety Act (OSHA), every employer in the United States has an obligation to provide a safe workplace for its employees. However, relatively few employers have established effective programs to combat violence in the workplace. Therefore, the purpose of this chapter is to provide security professionals, law enforcement personnel, employers, and employees with information on best practices to reduce workplace violence.

The types of incidents that occur at the workplace that generate great concern are:

- ❖ Verbal or written threats.
- ❖ Criminal acts against the company and employees.
- ❖ Various assaults (simple, aggravated).
- ❖ Acts of vandalism or sabotage.
- ❖ Stalking, trespassing, bomb threats, invasion of privacy
- ❖ Homicide or attempted homicides.
- ❖ Furtive gestures, such as brandishing or displaying a weapon.

GUIDELINES TO COMBATING WORKPLACE VIOLENCE

Organizations and corporations are experiencing unprecedented economic loses due to the phenomena of workplace violence such as, high costs of victims care and treatment. Employees are increasingly reporting abusive behaviors by coworkers, and less are being tolerated. Furthermore, managers, administrators and executives are no longer immune to acts of violence and employers have a legal obligation to provide protection. It is becoming widely acknowledged that simply the stressors of everyday life sometimes cause individuals to react inappropriately as they interact with others in the workplace resulting in friction. Obviously, the impact of threats and workplace violence are extraordinary, and security professionals must have an understanding of systematic guidelines and techniques necessary to minimize potential liabilities faced by the employer. Therefore, the following guidelines are recommended:

PRE-EMPLOYMENT SCREENING TECHNIQUES

To reduce the number of personnel prone to exhibiting violent behavior, employers should start the hiring process with effective pre-employment screening techniques.

- ❖ Include a waiver and release clause on job application forms.
- ❖ Check applicant's references and investigate any prior incidents of violence.
- ❖ Conduct thorough background checks and drug screening within the requirements of the employer.
- ❖ Vendors, service personnel, and contractors should also adhere to the host employer's security practices and policies.
- ❖ Request that legislative bodies make available the results of the criminal background investigation process.

COMMUNITY RESOURCES

Numerous programs and resources are available in the community that can assist employers in developing a comprehensive workplace violence plan. The following examples are expressed below:

❖ Invite local law enforcement to utilize businesses (to the extent it is possible) for report writing, breaks, etc., to promote interaction and good relations within the facility. Protocol can be explained at this stage regarding the proper actions during incidents involving threats and/or violence.

❖ Use security professionals and law enforcement to conduct training classes and workshops to educate employers and employees on preventing violence in the workplace.

❖ Keep abreast of the latest prevention and crime trend techniques, and communicate those findings to the employees.

REVIEW SECURITY PROCEDURES

Periodically review security policies and procedures, which will assist in minimizing the exposure to violence.

❖ Conduct threat assessments and security surveys of the facility to determine possible vulnerabilities.

❖ Use Crime Prevention Through Environmental Design (CPTED) concepts with all assessments.

❖ Monitor and control access to the facility by abnormal and former users (service personnel and former employees).

CREATE HOT-LINES OR ALERT PROCEDURES

❖ Create special lines of communication for key personnel as an emergency procedure.

❖ Post contact information of key personnel by name and/or number (fire, police, paramedics, etc.).

❖ Ensure that "evacuation" diagrams are posted on every floor of the facility.

IMPLEMENT A WORKPLACE VIOLENCE POLICY

❖ Establish a WPV policy that clearly states its intended purpose, such as drugs, weapons, and acts of violence.

❖ If violated, express the subsequent consequences (zero tolerance, formal discipline, etc.).

❖ Ensure that the policy is applicable to all employees and covers the entire facility.

IMPLEMENT PROPER TRAINING

❖ Initiate training programs for employees and management personnel in the proper procedures for handling various stages of discipline, changes in work environment, and terminations.

❖ Ensure that an Employee Assistance Program (EAP) is in place to assist employees and managers with sensitive matters of employment.

❖ Incidents of threats or violence regarding employees that occur outside the workplace should be reported to management personnel to prevent carryover into the workplace.

❖ Complete descriptions of person(s) and vehicle(s) should be provided to the proper security personnel at the workplace.

REDUCING THE THREAT

How do we reduce the threat of violence in the workplace? It is widely recommended among security professionals that all organizations adopt a zero tolerance policy against workplace violence. Furthermore, by developing and communicating key policies, and training management personnel to identify problem employees and situations, will help to achieve significant progress towards curtailing potentially serious incidents. Secondly, if problem employees begin to display *warning signs,* the employee must be immediately and appropriately addressed, since taking action at the time of the offense makes it much easier to prevent small incidents from escalating into a major crisis.

Particular attention should be given to employees who exhibit a change in behavior patterns and when the frequency and intensity of the behaviors are disruptive to the work environment. Additional *warning signs* are listed below:

- ❖ Constantly crying, sulking or throwing temper tantrums (anger issues).
- ❖ Excessive absenteeism or record of tardiness.
- ❖ Disregard for the health and safety of others, and shows disrespect towards authority.
- ❖ Evidence of increased mistakes or errors or unsatisfactory work quality, and refusal to acknowledge job performance issues.
- ❖ Faulty decision-making qualities and testing limits to see what will be tolerated.
- ❖ Constant swearing or emotional language, overreacting to criticism and making inappropriate statements.
- ❖ Forgetfulness, confusion and/or distractions, and the inability to focus.
- ❖ Makes excuses or blames others for mistakes, initiates complaints of unfair treatment.
- ❖ Complaints about the same problems repeatedly without resolving them, and insists that he or she is always right and never wrong.
- ❖ Misinterprets communication from supervisors or other employees.
- ❖ Social isolation and personal hygiene issues.
- ❖ Sudden and/or unpredictable changes in energy level, and complaints of unusual illnesses, without specifying the ailment(s).

Additionally, it is not always what a person actually says, but what their body is "doing." Therefore, to expand efforts to detect potentially violent employees, attention must be given to "non-verbal" cues or body language. The following ***physical (behavioral) warning signs*** are provided to assist employers in the screening process:

- ❖ Constant sweating, face turns extremely red, white or flustered.
- ❖ Pacing back and forth, very restless, has repetitive or escalated movements (similar to crack cocaine addicts).
- ❖ Increased use of drugs and/or alcohol.
- ❖ Constant trembling or shaking, observed with clenched jaws and/or fists.

❖ Getting too close when conversing, violating personal space.

❖ Staring into space or avoiding direct eye contact.

❖ Direct or veiled verbal threats or violent gestures.

❖ Is obsessed by a co-employee who does not share his/her interest (obsession is so intense that the co-employee may report the unwanted attention under a sexual harassment policy).

❖ Expresses extreme desperation over recent family, financial or personal problems.

❖ Talks loud or chants, projects change in voice tone.

❖ Is often a loner, obsessive involvement with the job, often with inconsistent performance, and no apparent outside interests.

❖ Scowling, shallow, rapid breathing, sneering or use of indecent language.

❖ Has an extreme interest in reading material where the subject is automatic or semi-automatic weapons.

❖ Displays overt, moral indignation in believing the employer is not following its own rules and procedures.

❖ Fascination with workplace violence incidents and expresses approval of using violence under similar circumstances.

❖ Engages in physical and/or verbal intimidation.

MANAGERS' CONDUCT TO REDUCE THE THREAT

There have been wars and rumors of wars regarding the personal conduct of managers while interacting with their subordinates. Experience dictates that the majority of potentially violent situations could have been greatly reduced if not eliminated, if supervisors and managers had prior training in sensitivity techniques. Unfortunately, there are far too many incidents where employees are already agitated by the time they meet with management. Therefore, the following guidelines are provided to assist management personnel in deescalating potentially violent employees in the workplace:

❖ Never promise the employee anything, but craft large problems into manageable solutions.

- ❖ Never entertain employee demands, but encourage the employee to provide their version or perspective of what occurred.
- ❖ Be mindful not to violate the employee's personal space, but create an accessible escape route if needed.
- ❖ Never use offensive language or come across too harsh, speak gently and calmly.
- ❖ Never use confusing or technical terms in confrontations, use clear and concise terminology.
- ❖ Never take sides or agree with issues that are contrary to policy or follow the letter-of-the-law, but repeat back what you believe is the question of concern.
- ❖ Never use furtive gestures, intimidating eye contact or challenging postures, assure the employee that their input is of value.
- ❖ Never downplay the criticality of the incident, or attempt to bargain with the employee, but calmly describe the consequences of the resultant behavior and allow a "cooling" period.
- ❖ Never use elevated tones when speaking and stand directly in front of the employee, but project a caring and tranquil posture.
- ❖ Never belittle, shame or criticize the employee, but acknowledge their feelings.

In the event that supervisors or managers respond to a potentially volatile incident, there are certain "calming phrases" that can be used to defuse an explosive situation:

- ❖ "Maybe you're right, however…"
- ❖ "If I have caused you any grief, please accept my sincere apology."
- ❖ "Would you like to have a seat and talk about this?"
- ❖ "This is the first I'm hearing of this, but if I can be of any assistance I will do my best to help."
- ❖ "Can you elaborate a little further as to what happened?"
- ❖ "I see that you're upset, please let me see if I can help."

If the behavior has escalated to a point of near explosion, try these helpful responses:

❖ If shouting or swearing – allow the employee to vent if it is not disruptive to others.

❖ If the employee is on the defensive – place the onus on them and allow them to consider reasonable options.

❖ If the employee is questioning procedure – express or reinforce company policy.

❖ If overt threatening – remove the employee immediately.

❖ If there is a noticeable change – point out that change and take appropriate action.

❖ If expressly agitated – acknowledge their emotion and allow a discussion of the matter.

❖ If employee flatly refuses a directive – have the employee suggest other option(s) and weigh the option(s).

12 RECOGNIZING EARLY WARNING SIGNS

We have already discussed some of the strategies for curtailing violence in the workplace, and will now turn the discussion to the concept of risk assessment. Risk is defined as the possibility of suffering harm or loss, and is surely another important area that employers should consider proactively when quantifying the loss potential caused by an act of violence. Moreover at this stage, security professionals can assist the organization in conducting a threat assessment or security analysis using the following three measures; 1) vulnerability – susceptibility to a particular act/loss; 2) probability – the likelihood of the act/loss occurring; 3) criticality – impact on the organization if the act/loss occurs. However, even without the benefit of a security professional's advice and counsel, it is important that management personnel begin to identify and assess the level of risk caused by various threats, and then determine if any action should be taken against potential violators. The following levels of risk are explained below:

- ❖ **Low Risk** – less serious or indirect threat, and requires prompt follow-up by management personnel: **1**
- ❖ **Low to Medium Risk** – somewhat serious threat, and requires immediate follow-up by management personnel: **2**
- ❖ **Medium Risk** – serious or more direct threat or behavior, and requires an investigation within one business day by management or security personnel: **3**

❖ **Medium to High Risk** – serious or direct threat, harm is probable and requires immediate investigation by security personnel: **4**

❖ **High Risk** – direct threat, imminent harm and danger to others, and requires immediate action by security personnel with possible involvement by local law enforcement: **5**

TABLETOP EXERCISES

Discuss and rate the following scenarios according to the aforementioned levels of risk:

A. "After work, my manager left in a great mood. She said she was in route to a fundraiser with the Governor and she was anxious to get there. As she entered the employee parking structure, she noticed that the windshield on her vehicle had been shattered. The next day, she said she had no idea who did it, so she asked us to come forward with a name and that no one would know. Instantly, I thought of Heather Lynn. On the evening it occurred, I was leaving the office and saw Heather in the restroom very angry about an email she had received. The email advised her that she was excessively tardy, and that her schedule would therefore be monitored by management. After I told Heather that she should try harder to arrive on time, she refused to accept it."

1	2	3	4	5
LOW RISK	LOW – MEDIUM RISK	MEDIUM RISK	MEDIUM – HIGH RISK	HIGH RISK

B. "Two weeks ago, Damon Lamar told me that he applied for a position in another department and the new position came with a salary increase, a company vehicle and a large bonus. Although he never mentioned anything further, this afternoon, I saw Damon leaving the manager's office and he looked furious. At the last break, he approached me and told me that Aubin Williams in Administration had stolen his position. His voice was very calm, but I could see that he was nearly in tears. He said since Aubin had stolen his position, he was going give Aubin a bullet between the eyes. He then told me it would be best that I not come to work tomorrow."

1	2	3	4	5
LOW RISK	LOW – MEDIUM RISK	MEDIUM RISK	MEDIUM – HIGH RISK	HIGH RISK

C. "I have been working with Clinise Wanette for about a year now. We never got together after work, but she would participate in occasional small talk during lunch hour. Last payday, she showed me a small .25 automatic weapon that was tucked into her handbag. She said it was fully loaded and bragged about how good it made her feel. I was shocked and begged her to put it away. However, she said I had nothing to worry about, and that the gun was for protection. I was puzzled as to why she needed protection at work."

1	2	3	4	5
LOW RISK	LOW – MEDIUM RISK	MEDIUM RISK	MEDIUM – HIGH RISK	HIGH RISK

D.   "Jamario was basically a loner and has always been very quiet, but lately he has been wearing suits and ties to work. Everyone in the Finance Department is talking about how he has developed a passion for Jaquita, the HR assistant. While we were on break the other day, Jaquita told me that Jamario has been sending her candy, gifts, and lengthy emails about how he worships the ground she walks on. She said that last Sunday he even showed up at her church and followed her home afterwards. She then started to cry and said she was finally going to tell Jamario that she was not interested and that he needs to get a life. Today, just before quitting time, Jamario stopped me in the hallway and told me that if he cannot have Jaquita, no one can! Then he asked me if I wanted his frequent flier miles he had been saving for years."

1	2	3	4	5
LOW RISK	LOW – MEDIUM RISK	MEDIUM RISK	MEDIUM – HIGH RISK	HIGH RISK

E.   "Andre has really been down on his luck this quarter. First, he came home early one day and caught his wife in bed with his best friend. Second, he recently found out that he is not the biological father of his youngest child. When you now see Andre, he stares into space and talks to himself. He never holds a conversation, and shows absolutely no emotion toward anyone or anything. He never goes out for lunch, and stays at work until midnight, probably because he has nowhere else to go. His breath reeks of alcohol; his hygiene needs extreme attention and his performance on the job leave much to be desired."

1	2	3	4	5
LOW RISK	LOW – MEDIUM RISK	MEDIUM RISK	MEDIUM – HIGH RISK	HIGH RISK

F.   "To me, Yusef is a very strange employee. He always reads magazines that feature exotic firearms, bombs, tanks, and weapons of mass destruction. At the last office party, he even showed up wearing military boots, fatigues and a toy MR-15. What is even stranger, Yusef's casual conversation always begins and ends with his fascination for the "afterlife." His actions have been so bazaar, that I voiced my concerns to my first line supervisor, but I have yet to receive a response."

1	2	3	4	5
LOW RISK	LOW – MEDIUM RISK	MEDIUM RISK	MEDIUM – HIGH RISK	HIGH RISK

COMPLETING THE WPV INVESTIGATIVE REPORT

Incidents of workplace violence in the form of threats, threatening behavior or overt acts of aggression, have been on the increase since the late twentieth century. In an attempt to prevent workplace violence and the resulting effects on tort and employment law, companies and institutions are encouraged to investigate all incidents of violence in the workplace. Therefore, the following investigative procedure is recommended to ensure that the necessary facts are properly conveyed and subsequently addressed:

PRELIMINARY PURPOSE AND SCOPE

- ❖ **Determine the initial offense** – review company policies and conduct regulations.
- ❖ **Collect the facts** – Interview the victim(s), explain the seriousness of the investigation; obtain specific details; determine the level and effect of the threat; ascertain if witnesses are available, secure names, dates and times; determine the validity of the complaint; if the victim(s) wishes to pursue the matter; and record the results in statement form. Interview witnesses (if any) to ascertain the description or identity of the victim(s) and perpetrator(s); obtain specific details and if a complaint exists; determine if the information is direct or hearsay; assess the credibility and validity of the information; and record the results in statement form. Interview alleged perpetrator(s), explain the content of the allegation; identify the level of the threat or act that is in question; determine if in fact a violation was committed; ask perpetrator(s) to respond to the violation-charges; ascertain if witnesses are available; assess the validity of the responses and record the results in statement form.

EVALUATE THE COLLECTED INFORMATION

❖ **Evaluate the information that was collected during the investigation** – evaluate the facts from an investigator's point of view; and differentiate the perpetrator's conduct from company policy violation(s).

❖ **Draft a thorough report** – using the following characteristics: <u>Timeliness</u> – ensures accurate report, <u>Accuracy</u> – validate all collected information, <u>Impartiality</u> – avoid an opinionated report, <u>Clarity</u> – use concise and well structured terminology, and <u>Relevance</u> – do not include information that has no bearing on the facts; draft the report in chronological order; detail when the complaint was first initiated; thoroughly detail the contents of the complaint; properly mark all attachments (exhibits); detail the results of all interviews; document if information is direct or hearsay; provide evidence that sustains or refutes the allegation; detail what policy violation(s) occurred, justifying corrective action; use caution when recommending discipline (disposition should be left with management or Human Resources).

❖ **Submit report** – to upper management, Human Resources (HR), and to local law enforcement if warranted.

13 SCHOOL SAFETY AND SECURITY

Schools contend with issues of violence like never before, and its effect on society at large has been sometimes overwhelming. School violence can include emotional and physical ridicule or bullying, staff assaults, threats, arsons/fires, sexual offenses, drugs/alcohol, weapons, as well as graffiti, vandalism, breaking and entering, and gangs. The Jeanne Clery Act (originally known as the Campus Security Act), was a landmark case which gave rise to a federal mandate that requires colleges and universities across the United States to disclose information about crime on and around their schools. The following procedures can be a valuable tool to identify, decrease and/or curtail criminal activities, and provide procedures for a successful outcome for those responding to school emergencies:

POST INCIDENT COUNSELING

Post incident counseling consists of a group or single professional counselor(s) trained in handling critical or sensitive matters, who can assist victims or witnesses in dealing with traumatic incidents. Counselors generally allow the affected individuals to talk about the incident after it has occurred, without judgment or criticism. Successful counseling can minimize the chances that involved persons will develop or suffer from post-traumatic stress disorder (PTSD). PTSD is defined as a severe anxiety disorder that can develop after exposure to any event that causes psychological trauma. This disorder can lead to or enhance the threat of suicide or homicide after the overwhelmed individual's ability to cope is increasingly diminished. To implement post incident counseling, the following procedures are recommended:

- ❖ Determine the level and extent of counseling needed for the involved parties.
- ❖ Identify specific locations where counseling should take place.
- ❖ Assess stress levels and determine if follow-up is necessary.
- ❖ Provide counseling for victim(s) and those who are closely acquainted with the victim(s).
- ❖ Identify key personnel who will coordinate counseling and/or attend support-activities such as doctor/hospital visits, churches, or funerals.
- ❖ Allow students or staff extra time to makeup missed assignments or examinations.

DEMONSTRATIONS

Student protests can best be avoided by early recognition of volatile issues on school grounds and in the surrounding communities. A concerted effort to report all concerns to security personnel and school administrators is highly recommended. Even though students have a right to free speech, they cannot interfere or hamper the educational experience for others. In the event that an unauthorized demonstration occurs:

- ❖ Notify the school administrator or principal and Safety/Security Department if available.
- ❖ Provide the description and exact location of the disturbance.
- ❖ Provide information relative to the instigators, number of participants and the issue at hand.
- ❖ Never attempt to remove or suppress unruly participants without additional assistance.
- ❖ To prevent sabotage, make sure vital records and important files are well secured.
- ❖ Safety/Security Department personnel, school administrators or local law enforcement shall be responsible to restore order.
- ❖ Widely communicate the consequences for violating any school code of conduct rules.

❖ Station adequate school administrators at the perimeters of the disturbance, to provide the necessary "eyes and ears" if future testimony is needed.

❖ Control media information.

BREAKING AND ENTERING (B&E)

The term breaking and entering (B&E) relative to schools refers to an unauthorized entry into a school building or institution when the school is closed (after hours, weekends, holidays, and school vacations). In the event that a school or institution is broken into:

❖ Do not enter the facility prior to the arrival of local law enforcement (the police).

❖ Do not touch anything or use the telephone.

❖ Immediately contact your Safety/Security Department, local law enforcement, and then the principal or school administrator (with personal cell or telephone off-premise).

❖ List all missing items and secure facility after it is released by local law enforcement.

❖ Conduct security/threat assessment and subsequent CPTED target hardening techniques.

TRESPASSERS/INTRUDERS

An intruder is one who knowingly enters school property without a legitimate reason, and can pose a threat. This could include person(s) with weapons, someone whose intention may be to abduct a student or staff member, etc. To effectively deal with the problem, the following procedure is recommended:

❖ Notify the school administrator or principal and Safety/Security Department if available.

❖ Request additional assistance prior to approaching the subject(s).

❖ In a non-threatening manner, progress to an introduction, and determine the purpose of the subject's visit.

❖ Ask the subject to come to the administrative office to confirm or deny entry.

❖ If the subject has no legitimate business, request that the subject leave, and accompany him/her to the nearest exit.

❖ If the subject refuses to leave, state the consequences, which include notifying the police.

❖ If subject still refuses, immediately leave the area if there is a potential for violence, call 911, Safety/Security Department, and principal or school administrator.

❖ Provide full description and circumstances to police, and make subsequent notifications to school administrators.

HOSTAGE SITUATIONS

Although not common occurrences, schools are occasionally the location of hostage situations. The deadliest occurred in Beslan, Russia in 2004, where terrorists held the school under siege for 53 hours before a shootout resulted in the deaths of more than 360 people. Hostage incidents recorded in Bailey, Colorado and Nickel Mines, Pennsylvania, also resulted in tragedy. Therefore, school administrators should become familiar with best practices for handling an event of this nature:

❖ Call 911 (local law enforcement) immediately, if possible, and provide details of the situation at hand.

❖ If the hostage taker is unaware that others are present, do not attempt any action, but seal off the area near the scene.

❖ Notify the Crisis Intervention Team, Safety/Security Department, and school administrators.

❖ Give control of the scene to local law enforcement and the crisis team.

❖ If taken as a hostage, try to remain calm, do not quarrel with the taker, and follow all instructions, except (if at all possible) consenting to being taken away from the facility.

❖ Collect detailed notes of the incident, which might be used for future testimony.

❖ Provide post incident counseling if requested.

STUDENT RELEASING PROCEDURES

The security and wellbeing of students are of the utmost importance. The unauthorized removal of a student or the disclosure of student information is strictly prohibited. Therefore, for the safety and protection of all students, visitors must always be directed to the administration office before proceeding to a classroom. This includes parents or other relatives of the student. No student will be permitted to leave the building with a visitor (including parents) unless the circumstances are verified. Also, pay close attention to the following:

❖ Keep abreast of all students with special custody arrangements (social services and/or court ordered situations).
❖ Confirm validity with agency, parent or guardian, prior to the release of any student.
❖ Verify the identification of the person requesting the release of a student, from photo source.
❖ If the student reveals signs of reluctance, do not authorize the release and hold the student in the administration office, until all matters of interest are addressed.
❖ Verify court documents through true copies.
❖ If unauthorized release occurs, contact the school administrators immediately.
❖ If unauthorized release is confirmed by senior administrator, contact local law enforcement and Safety/Security Department.
❖ Provide full description of the perpetrator(s) and other emergency information to local law enforcement.
❖ Control media information.

VANDALISM/MALICIOUS DESTRUCTION OF PROPERTY

Laws prohibit students from destroying or defacing any school building, facility or property. This includes property belonging to, rented by, or property that is on loan to the school system, and property belonging to school employees or other students. If responding to a possible incident of property destruction, the following procedure is recommended:

❖ Immediately contact school administrators.
❖ Assess the damage and ascertain how the incident took place.
❖ If minor damage exists under a less serious offense, administrators will determine if local law enforcement and Safety/Security Department should be contacted.
❖ If damages occurred from felonious actions, contact local law enforcement and Safety/Security Department, and provide assistance to locate possible suspects and/or witnesses.
❖ Make post notifications to senior administrator and maintenance staff if necessary.

SHELTERING/SAFE LOCATIONS

Sheltering can provide safe havens for students and the community during emergencies (weather, natural or nuclear disasters, etc.). Shelters or safe havens should be previously designated and determined by the type of emergency that occurs, along with the following recommendations:

❖ Assign locations within each facility located on school grounds.
❖ School administrator initiates order to assemble, and coordinate the orderly passage of all students.
❖ Faculty and staff should ensure that all students are accounted for per the class rosters.
❖ Depending upon the type of emergency, all doors and windows should be well secured.
❖ Perishables should be placed in proper storage containers and refrigerated if necessary.
❖ Make medical supplies, first aid, and emergency kits available.
❖ School administrators and/or emergency responders only, are responsible for giving the "all clear" signal.

STUDENT DISTURBANCES

School disturbances can range from mischievous behavior to full blown physical assaults against classmates or teachers. Disturbances can contribute to low academic achievement, cause damage to student relationships and lessen community support. Therefore, even the simplest disruptions should be addressed at the early stages to prevent escalation into more serious incidents. To assist in diminishing disturbances, administrators may wish to develop support groups such as peer mediation, business and parental interventions, and even extra incentives for teachers to promote a "we care" environment. However, in the event trouble does develop, the following procedure might prove useful:

❖ Sound the "alarm code" signal if warranted (a system of warning or alarm codes should have been previously devised to alert school administrators in the event of serious incidents such as disturbances, lock-down, shootings, etc.).

❖ Identify the location of the disturbance and the person(s) involved.

❖ Notify school administrators, the Safety/Security Department, and local law enforcement if necessary.

❖ Attempt to maintain calm, and meet with other administrators, student representatives, and law enforcement personnel.

❖ All classroom doors should be locked and secured.

❖ Students should not be released until instructed by school administrators or the "all clear" signal is given.

❖ Document and collect detailed notes of the incident, which may be used in a court of law.

THEFT/LARCENY

Theft/larceny is defined as the unauthorized taking, carrying, riding away, or concealing the property of another person, including motor driven vehicles, without threat, violence, or bodily harm. If committed on the grounds of a school, college or university, the following guidelines will prove useful:

❖ Immediately contact school administrators.

❖ Assess the stolen item(s) and ascertain how the larceny took place.

❖ If item(s) of lesser value was taken, school administrators will determine if local law enforcement and Safety/Security Department should be notified.

❖ If item(s) of increased value was/were taken, contact local law enforcement and Safety/Security Department, and provide assistance to locate possible suspects and/or witnesses.
❖ Make post notification to senior administrator.

ROBBERY/EXTORTION

Robbery is defined as the unauthorized taking or attempting to take the property of another by use of force, threats or intimidation. Robbery is usually divided into different categories or classifications such as <u>unarmed</u>, <u>armed</u>, and <u>extortion</u>. <u>Unarmed robbery</u> is committed without a weapon; <u>armed robbery</u> is committed when the perpetrator uses a weapon or anything that represents a weapon; <u>extortion</u> is committed when one threatens another for the purpose of securing money or property, or to compel another to commit an act against their will. If an act of robbery/extortion occurs on school grounds, security professionals recommend the following:

❖ Notify the school administrator or principal, and Safety/Security Department, if available.
❖ Provide the details and exact location of the incident, and determine if a weapon was used.
❖ The school administrator or Safety/Security Department will determine if local law enforcement should be notified.
❖ Provide information relative to the descriptions and roles of all subjects involved.
❖ Safety/Security Department personnel, school administrators or local law enforcement, will take the necessary actions to calm all victims involved.
❖ Make post notifications to additional personnel and/or departments per the advice of local law enforcement.
❖ Provide post incident counseling if requested.

WEAPONS VIOLATIONS

In the event a subject is suspected of carrying a weapon on their person, in a book bag, purse or any other container, the following steps should be implemented:

❖ Notify the school administrator or principal, and Safety/Security Department, if available.

❖ Provide the details and exact location of the subject, and assess the credibility of the reported information.

❖ The school administrator or Safety/Security Department will determine if local law enforcement should be notified.

❖ Seek additional assistance from staff and/or administrators, and approach the subject.

❖ If no direct threat of a weapon exists, escort the subject to the administration office and make sure he/she is isolated.

❖ Advise the subject of the allegation and question him/her regarding the type and location of the weapon(s).

❖ Advise local law enforcement of the details and provide assistance if requested to conduct a search.

❖ If a weapon is located, it will be secured by local law enforcement.

❖ If the subject barricades himself/herself, treat the incident as an armed or hostage situation.

❖ Make post notifications to additional personnel and/or departments per the advice of local law enforcement.

❖ Document and collect detailed notes of the incident, which may be used in court as future testimony.

Whenever a person(s) has a weapon, or is holding another against their will, the following action is recommended:

❖ Immediately notify the school administrator or principal, and Safety/Security Department, and advise if a weapon was observed.

❖ If weapon is confirmed, notify Crisis Intervention Team and local law enforcement.

❖ Provide identity and location of the suspect, but do not approach. From a distance, request the evacuation of the classroom (only if the suspect is isolated and contained). All other neighboring classrooms should be locked and secured.

❖ Secure suspect's emergency information from the administration office, and ask the subject to go to a predetermined assembly area. If he/she refuses, await the arrival of local law enforcement.

❖ If weapon is visible, shots were fired or suspect is brandishing a weapon in a threatening manner, sound the alert code. The code should have a predetermined instruction related to the type of alert dispatched.

❖ If the suspect is a student, contact the immediate family member(s).

❖ When local law enforcement arrives, they will take charge of the scene.

❖ Document and collect detailed notes of the incident, which might be used in court as future testimony.

❖ Refer media to the appropriate spokesperson.

❖ Provide post incident counseling if requested.

If the incident involves a "drive-by shooting", the following action is recommended:

❖ After the first sound of gunfire, instruct all students to drop to the floor.

❖ Stay secured until a move to a safer location can be accomplished, and then identify the problem.

❖ Notify the school administrators and the Safety/Security Department. A senior administrator determines if local law enforcement should be contacted.

❖ Search for possible injured person(s) and assess the damages.

❖ If a student has been shot, immediately contact 911, local law enforcement, Safety/Security Department, and Emergency Medical Service (EMS).

❖ Locate possible witnesses, and attempt to identify perpetrator(s). Isolate the witnesses and prevent idle conversation.

❖ Once local law enforcement arrives, they will take charge of the scene.

❖ If the incident results in a death, local law enforcement will control the entire investigation.

❖ Assist local law enforcement with identifying suspects and possible victims from emergency information provided by the administration office.
❖ Document and collect detailed notes of the incident, which may be used in a court as future testimony.
❖ Complete notification procedures, including senior administrators, concerned parents and/or guardians.
❖ Refer media to the appropriate spokesperson.
❖ Initiate post incident counseling procedures for students, staff, and administrators, if requested.

ARSON/FIRE/EXPLOSION

Fires and explosions can cause deadly results if alert-procedures are not properly maintained. Fires are caused by the rapid oxidation of a material in the chemical process of combustion; while explosions are rapid increases in volume and the release of energy in an extreme manner, that usually generate high temperatures and the release of extreme gases. If fires and explosions are intentionally set, the act is classified as arson. Arson is the crime of intentionally or maliciously setting fire to structures, the property of another or to one's own property to collect insurance compensation. Arson, fire, or explosions that occur in a school setting, are extremely hazardous, and have high potential for loss.

If a fire, smoke, odor of gas or explosion is detected, the following action is recommended:

❖ Activate the alarm.
❖ Evacuate the building and direct all personnel to a pre-determined assembly area, by the most direct route.
❖ If the normal route is too hazardous, use the public address system (P.A.) to broadcast an alternate route or assembly area to be used.
❖ Class attendance rosters should be used to account for all students.
❖ School administrators will notify the local fire department or fire marshal.

- ❖ Pre-appointed staff should conduct a search for additional students, and report those who are still missing.
- ❖ Prepare to move students to another location as not to interfere with emergency service equipment or personnel.
- ❖ If a fire is the result of arson, assist local law enforcement and fire investigators in their investigation; help identify any possible suspects and/or witnesses.
- ❖ Allow no one to re-enter the facility until the scene is cleared by fire or law enforcement authorities.
- ❖ Implement post incident counseling provisions for students, staff and administrators, if requested.

NUCLEAR DISASTER

As the United States continues to face various world crises, the subject regarding nuclear disasters is gaining momentum. In case of nuclear attack, the Emergency Alert System (EAS) was put in place to provide disaster related warning to the nation's citizens. The EAS is a national public warning system that requires broadcasters, cable television systems, wireless cable systems, satellite digital audio radio service providers, and direct broadcast satellite providers, to provide communications capability to the President, which will allow him/her to address the American public during a national emergency. Even though the EAS would likely have been initiated, if a nuclear attack occurred in the U.S., the following procedures are recommended for schools, colleges and universities:

- ❖ If students are initially outside the facility, direct them inside to the lowest level away from windows and flying objects, such as a basement or tunnel. If no cover is available, direct them to lie down on the ground in a curled position, or kneel in a duck-and-cover position.
- ❖ If students are initially inside the facility, direct them to the lowest level away from windows and flying objects.
- ❖ If a basement is not available, seek cover in a hallway or inner room.

❖ Close all doors and tape plastic sheeting, aluminum foil or waxed paper over vents, electrical outlets, and exhaust fans.

❖ Seal under all doors with wet towels or clothing, and if time permits, shut down gas, water, and electrical service to buildings that will be used for shelters.

❖ Collect food, water, a first aid kit, and portable battery operated radio, and immediately tune in a news station.

❖ Avoid using elevators, as they will draw air from the outside while in motion.

❖ Remain as calm as possible and do not panic, and await further instructions from school administrators.

❖ If no "all clear signal" is heard, remain in the shelter and be guided by the advice of the radio station personnel.

EVACUATION PROCEDURES

Depending upon the type of emergency, an evacuation order may be given by way of a continual emergency alert signal or by word of mouth. In the event that an evacuation order is given, the following procedure is recommended:

❖ Contact local law enforcement if warranted.

❖ The Emergency Response Team, consisting of a member of the school administrators, should determine if evacuation is needed and if alternate locations will be used.

❖ Modes of transportation should be made available if requested.

❖ Evacuate the building and direct all personnel to a predetermined assembly area, by the most direct route.

❖ If the normal route is too hazardous, use the P.A. announcement to broadcast an alternate route or assembly area to be used.

❖ Secure all windows and doors, and disable all utility equipment at the facility.

❖ School administrators and/or staff should have class rosters available to account for all students.

❖ Assign a member of the school administrator's team to ensure that all students have evacuated the facility.

❖ Notify a senior school administrator if students are missing.

BOMB THREAT

Even though the majority of bomb threats are hoaxes (2% - 5% are real), care and caution should be used when receiving information that a bomb has been planted inside the school, or on school grounds. It is important to note that although bomb threats are generally received via telephone, threats that are written, e-mailed, or sent by facsimile, cannot be ignored. The following instructions are recommended once a bomb threat has been received:

❖ If by telephone, keep the caller on the line as long as possible by asking repeated questions.
❖ Notify school administrators, the Safety/Security Department, and local law enforcement, as soon as possible.
❖ Use a Bomb Threat Checklist to assist with documenting all necessary information from the caller.
❖ A Bomb Threat Checklist is used as a reference to record pertinent information while receiving a bomb threat.
❖ Ask for the location, possible time of detonation, and reason for planting the bomb.
❖ Ascertain the caller's gender, age, race, voice pattern, and type of speech (accents or impediments).
❖ Make notes of everything the caller said and the exact wording of the threat.
❖ Listen for background noises that can possibly identify the caller. Engines running, foreign languages, music, and weather conditions, are all noises that can be fruitful.
❖ Await the arrival of local law enforcement, brief them thoroughly, and surrender the operation to them.
❖ Supply keys and equipment to assist local law enforcement in building searches.
❖ Staff should be equipped with class rosters to account for all students.
❖ Do not wait for the police to order the evacuation of the building; order a full evacuation when the caller is credible and the location of the bomb is unknown.

- ❖ Do not use main entrances for evacuation unless it is necessary.
- ❖ Provide an attendance list to school administrators. Select key administrators and staff to serve as search teams to assist local law enforcement.
- ❖ Local law enforcement will contact the Bomb Squad (specialized unit), who manage the search.
- ❖ Do not attempt under any circumstances to remove a suspected bomb, this will be handled by bomb disposal personnel only.
- ❖ Do not touch suspicious or unusual packages, or objects.
- ❖ Direct all personnel to a pre-determined assembly area, by the most direct route.
- ❖ Do not use radios, cell phones or other electronic devices, as they can detonate bombs.
- ❖ After evacuation, allow no one to reenter the facility.
- ❖ Assign a member of the school administrator's team to ensure that all students have evacuated the facility.
- ❖ Notify senior school administrator if students are missing.
- ❖ A senior administrator will advise all school administrators of the "all clear" to resume normal operations.
- ❖ Complete an incident report for future reference.

BOMB THREAT CHECKLIST

Date:_____   Time:_____

Threat received from:_____(written, email, fax, other)

Exact words used by Caller:_____
_____
_____
_____
_____

QUESTIONS TO ASK

1. When will the bomb explode?_____
2. Where is the bomb right now?_____
3. How many bombs are there?_____
4. Can you give a description of the bomb?_____
5. What kind of bomb is it?_____
6. Who placed the bomb?_____
7. Why?_____
8. What is your name?_____
9. Where are you calling from?_____

CALLER'S VOICE DESCRIPTIONS

☐ Calm	☐ Slow	☐ Nasal	☐ Angry	☐ Broke	☐ Rapid
☐ Stutter	☐ Disguised	☐ Lisp	☐ Sincere	☐ Rapid	☐ Giggler
☐ Deep	☐ Crying	☐ Squeaky	☐ Excited	☐ Stressed	☐ Accent
☐ Slurred	☐ Normal	☐ Loud	☐ Soft	☐ Raspy	☐ Familiar
☐ Male	☐ Female	☐ Young	☐ Middle Age	☐ Old	☐ Other

Remarks:_____

Background Sounds:_____
_____

Time Caller Hung Up:_____

Person Receiving Call:_____ Position_____

Address:_____ Phone #_____

Call Immediately Reported To:_____ Phone #_____

PHYSICAL ASSAULTS/FIGHTS

In accordance with the First Amendment to the United States Constitution, students have the right to express their beliefs in the form of free speech, and they have protection under the law while so doing. With that being said, students do not have the right to shout fire in a crowed theatre (this is illegal), or to engage in disorderly conduct that hinders the ability of others to pursue an education. In as much as the First Amendment provides for certain protections and upholds certain rights, it should not be used as an excuse to engage in raucous disagreements, discord, and conflicts that result in danger to others. Although educational institutions go to great lengths to ensure student safety, they are not always successful, and sometimes there will be circumstances that lead to physical fighting and assaults.

In the event that physical assaults occur on school grounds (this includes colleges and universities), the following procedures are recommended:

❖ If the suspect(s) uses a weapon, the victim(s) or suspect(s) sustains an injury that requires medical attention, the victim is a member of the administrative staff, or the victim alleges injury, immediately contact local law enforcement.
❖ Ensure that students and staff are safe.
❖ Notify the school administrator or principal and Safety/Security Department, if available.
❖ Attempt to make contact with a calm demeanor, and identify the problem.
❖ Determine if the Emergency Medical Service (EMS) should be dispatched to the scene.
❖ Isolate and close off the area where the incident is taking place.
❖ Attempt to clear the area of other students to reduce on-lookers and decrease danger.
❖ Escort the students to the administration office and keep them as calm as possible.
❖ Advise local law enforcement of the details and provide assistance to identify possible suspect(s) or victim(s), if requested.

❖ Make post notifications to additional personnel and/or departments per the advice of local law enforcement.
❖ Implement post incident counseling procedures for students, staff, and administrators, if requested.
❖ Document and collect detailed notes of the incident, which might be used in court as future testimony.

SEXUAL ASSAULT

Sexual assaults involve various degrees of Criminal Sexual Conduct (CSC), ranging from "acquaintance rape" (date rape) to "statutory rape." Criminal Sexual Assault is the act of forcible sexual penetration by one person upon another. Incest, rape, attempted rape, and unwanted sexual touching of one's genitalia, are all classified under sexual assault. Acquaintance rape is the act of forcible sexual penetration, or penetration after one has been rendered defenseless by the use of some form of narcotic, and committed by someone the victim knows. Although labeled acquaintance rape in most states, the actual crime is covered under the criminal sexual assault statutes.

Statutory rape is described as engaging in sexual activity where one participant is below the legal age required to consent to the behavior, and generally refers to sex between an adult and a sexually mature minor past the age of puberty.

In the event that a sexual assault occurs on or near school property, the following procedures are recommended:

❖ Immediately notify the school administrator and the Safety/Security Department.
❖ Locate, identify, and remain with the victim.
❖ Contact local law enforcement.
❖ Do not allow the victim to shower, bathe, wash, douche, or attempt to clean up.
❖ Do not allow the victim to change clothes.
❖ Instruct the victim not to urinate, as traces of drugs can be found in urine.

❖ If the victim drank from a glass or can, save it for local law enforcement, along with the offender's glass.

❖ Discourage discussion between other students.

❖ Identify the alleged perpetrator and release all acquired information to local law enforcement.

❖ Assist local law enforcement with emergency information from student files, and after additional requests.

❖ Notify parent(s) and/or guardian(s).

❖ Make post notifications to administrators, additional personnel and/or departments, per local law enforcement.

❖ Local law enforcement will recommend counseling agencies and/or contact with the National Crime Victim Hotline.

❖ Document and collect detailed notes of the incident, which might be used in court as future testimony.

❖ Complete necessary incident report(s).

TRANSPORTATION INCIDENT

In the event of a serious incident during school transportation on buses or other modes of travel, the safety of the students and school personnel are most important. The trip director must ensure that he/she has access to emergency instructions during all school-sanctioned events and if a serious accident or incident occurs, the following procedure is recommended:

❖ The trip director checks for the extent of injuries.

❖ The trip director establishes lines of communication with school administrators to provide perpetual updates regarding the incident.

❖ Notify 911, local law enforcement, or EMS, to report the accident or incident.

❖ Administer first aid if necessary.

❖ Safely secure the vehicle and display the appropriate portable warning signs.

❖ Remove students away from imminent threat to a safe location.

❖ The student roster should account for all students, and updates should be provided when available.
❖ Request that the health information of concerned student(s) be provided by the administration office.
❖ Contact parent(s) or guardian(s) regarding the injured and the location of the medical facility if conveyed.
❖ An alternate means of transportation for the remaining students should be provided.
❖ Document and collect detailed notes of the incident.

CRITICAL INJURY/DEATH/POISONING

In the event of critical injuries due to illness and intentional or accidental acts, the response may vary according to the circumstances that caused the incident. However, it is important that all appropriate personnel be informed and that pertinent information be disseminated in a sensitive and confidential manner in order to alleviate any further distress to students, relatives, and staff. Whether the incident takes place on or off school property, the following procedure is recommended:

❖ Identify the problem and location.
❖ Immediately notify the school administrator or principal, Crisis Intervention Team and Safety/Security Department, if available.
❖ The Crisis Intervention Team or school administrators will determine if local law enforcement should be notified.
❖ Notify the Emergency Response Team, which should include a school administrator.
❖ If necessary, seek additional assistance from staff to identify victim(s), witnesses or perpetrator(s).
❖ Collect victim(s) medical history, contact information, and other pertinent information from the administration office.
❖ Administer first aid, such as controlling bleeding, ensure breathing, keeping victim warm, ensuring that the victim is not moved or loosening constricting clothing.
❖ Discourage discussion, and attempt to calm and remove students from the incident location.

- ❖ If student(s) ingested poison, identify the substance, save the container, and contact the American Association of Poison Control Center.
- ❖ Ascertain emergency information of injured student(s); notify parent(s) or guardian(s) and/or emergency contact person(s), and additional staff member(s) if requested.
- ❖ Provide the location of the medical facility if conveyed.
- ❖ Assist local law enforcement with details, and provide assistance if requested to identify possible suspect(s), witnesses or additional victim(s).
- ❖ Make post notifications to additional personnel and/or departments per the recommendation of local law enforcement.
- ❖ Implement post incident counseling procedures for students, staff and administrators, if requested.
- ❖ Complete necessary incident report(s).
- ❖ Refer the media to the appropriate spokesperson.

If a death or homicide occurs:

- ❖ Verify that the incident resulted in a death and identify the location.
- ❖ Immediately contact 911, local law enforcement, Safety/Security Department, and the Emergency Medical Service (EMS).
- ❖ Notify the school administrator or principal, the Crisis Intervention Team, and Safety/Security Department, if available.
- ❖ Search for possible additional injured person(s) and assess the damages.
- ❖ Locate possible witnesses, and attempt to identify perpetrator(s). Isolate the witnesses and prevent idle conversation.
- ❖ Once local law enforcement arrives, they will take charge of the scene.
- ❖ Assist local law enforcement with identifying suspects and possible victims from emergency information provided by the administration office.
- ❖ Document and collect detailed notes of the incident, which might be used in court as future testimony.

❖ Local law enforcement will determine if additional notifications are to be made, including senior administrators, concerned parents and/or guardians.

❖ Refer the media to the appropriate spokesperson.

❖ Initiate post incident counseling procedures for students, staff and administrators, if requested.

HAZARDOUS ACCIDENT/CHEMICAL SPILL

A hazardous accident may occur on or near schools, colleges and universities, which can be an extreme threat to students, staff, and administrators. Threats can include accidents from nearby chemical establishments, broken fuel lines, and overturned tankers. Types of hazardous materials are explosives, hazardous gases, flammable solids, oxidizers, or toxic infectious substances. Chemical spills include a variety of hazardous chemical agents that, when released, could harm the health of students and staff. The spills can occur at school laboratories or near the facility, much like hazardous materials. Chemicals can be corrosive, toxic, and may react often explosively. The impact of chemical accidents can be deadly for both humans and the environment. Therefore, if chemical spills or hazardous accidents occur inside the school, the following procedures are recommended:

❖ Contact 911, local law enforcement, school administrators, the Safety/Security Department, Fire Department, and the Office of Hazardous Materials Safety (HAZMAT).

❖ Evacuate the facility if fumes are nauseous, irritating to the eyes, or if breathing is difficult.

❖ Assign a member of the school administrator's team to ensure that all students have evacuated the facility.

❖ Notify the senior school administrator if students are missing.

❖ The administrator or Safety/Security Department will take charge of the scene until HAZMAT and/or Fire arrives.

❖ If the spill is in a laboratory, isolate the area, and close all doors.

❖ Remove ignition sources, unplug all electrical equipment, and initiate exhaust ventilation.

- ❖ Move victim(s) from the immediate area.
- ❖ Remove contaminated clothing; wash exposed skin with cold running water, or shower if possible.
- ❖ Use protective equipment while containing the spill.
- ❖ Wet mop the area until hazardous waste personnel arrives.
- ❖ Fire or HAZMAT will determine post-evacuation sheltering if required.
- ❖ If ingested, identify the substance and contact the Centers for Disease Control and Prevention (CDC) for instructions and treatment.
- ❖ If chemicals are in the eyes, wash with running water for no less than 15 minutes, and seek immediate medical attention.
- ❖ Administer first aid and follow-up with medical attention.
- ❖ Contact parents and provide medical status.
- ❖ Fire and/or HAZMAT will determine when to resume operations.
- ❖ Complete necessary incident report(s).
- ❖ Refer the media to the appropriate spokesperson.
- ❖ Make post notifications to additional personnel and/or departments, per recommendation of Fire or HAZMAT.
- ❖ Implement post incident counseling procedures for students, staff, and administrators, if requested.

If chemical spills or hazardous accidents occur outside or near the school, the following procedure is then recommended:

- ❖ The Fire Department and HAZMAT will determine if the facility requires evacuating or shelter-locations, and notification of the school administrator.
- ❖ Fire will take charge of the scene and recommend sheltering, evacuation or further action.
- ❖ If ordered to evacuate, assign a member of the school administrator's team to ensure that all students have evacuated the facility.
- ❖ Notify the senior school administrator if students are missing.
- ❖ Notify parents of the incident status.

❖ Move person(s) who are in danger of becoming contaminated crosswind from the source of the hazard, since the wind could be carrying dangerous fumes.
❖ Complete the necessary incident report(s).
❖ Make post notifications to additional personnel and/or departments, per recommendation of Fire or HAZMAT.
❖ Implement post incident counseling procedures for students, staff, and administrators, if requested.
❖ Refer the media to the appropriate spokesperson.

ALCOHOLIC LIQUOR/TOBACCO

The basic premise of the American educational system is to provide every student, not only a quality education, but also a safe environment in which to learn. Although studies show that most students avoid the unsafe use of alcohol, tobacco, and other drugs, some are influenced by the high-risk behaviors of their peers. Binges with alcohol that include tobacco, causes respiratory problems even cancer, and can lead to tragic results. Deaths from alcohol poisoning and alcohol-related incidents have occurred in and near schools at staggering rates, and therefore call for implementation of a zero tolerance policy regarding illegal alcoholic liquor and minors in possession of tobacco.

In most states, alcoholic liquor includes any beverage containing .05% or more of alcohol by volume, and cannot be possessed by anyone under the age of 21. Alcohol content less than .05% by volume, such as so-called "non-alcoholic beer", cannot be possessed by anyone under the age of 18. Tobacco products include cigarettes, cigars, chewing tobacco, snuff or pipe tobacco, or tobacco in any form and are a misdemeanor if possessed by anyone under the age of 18. If violations are encountered, the following action is recommended:

❖ Notify the principal or school administrator if on school property.
❖ Identify the problem, inform the student of the offense, and escort the student to the administration office.
❖ School administrators should always approach in pairs.

❖ Collect evidence such as containers and butts, and notify parent(s) and/or guardian(s).
❖ If a serious offense, contact local law enforcement.
❖ Notify the school senior administrator, and/or additional staff if necessary.
❖ Complete necessary incident report(s).

DRUGS/NARCOTICS

The abundance of messages from advertisers that constantly bombard today's youth with glamorous ads featuring alcohol and cigarettes are relentless, and for some, may well be one of the contributing factors leading to vulnerability to substance abuse. Fortunately, studies have found that most teens do not use drugs, however, for those who do; a single use can have adverse effects on the mind. Some of the effects of drug use include but are not limited to, clouded judgment and unwise decision-making, which can lead to accidents, irate behavior, poor performance in school, and more importantly, the risk of overdose and ultimate death.

Drug sales are also problematic in and around schools. As society has become increasingly materialistic, some students become overly influenced by ad campaigns that hype the so-called status that comes with owning particular products. These students view selling drugs as the fastest way to get cash to purchase the expensive goods and services viewed by the culture as desirable.

If issues with drugs and/or narcotics arise, the following procedures are recommended:

❖ Identify the problem and evaluate the findings.
❖ Regarding drug use or overdose, immediately notify the principal, school administrator and the Safety/Security Department.
❖ The school administrator or Safety/Security Department will determine if local law enforcement should be contacted.
❖ Identify the victim/perpetrator from administrative office files, secure the emergency information, and remove the student from class.

- ❖ Keep the student quiet and calm, and await the arrival of local law enforcement.
- ❖ Discourage discussion between other students in class.
- ❖ If an emergency exists, notify the Emergency Medical Service (EMS), and provide the type of drug, quantity, time and method the drug was taken.
- ❖ Provide local law enforcement with emergency information and assist with additional requests.
- ❖ Notify the parent(s) and/or guardian(s), or emergency contact person(s).
- ❖ Make post notifications to administrator, additional personnel, and/or departments, per the recommendation of local law enforcement.
- ❖ Document and collect detailed notes of the incident, which might be used in court as future testimony.
- ❖ Complete necessary incident report(s).

Regarding drug sales or possession, the following procedure is recommended:

- ❖ Identify the problem and evaluate the findings.
- ❖ Assess the credibility of the reported information.
- ❖ Assess administrative files and witness information relative to the character, activities, and scholastic achievement of the suspect(s).
- ❖ Notify the principal, school administrator and the Safety/Security Department, of your results.
- ❖ Assess the school policy for search and seizure guidelines in your district to determine the elements of probable cause.
- ❖ If drugs are located, advise the Safety/Security Department and local law enforcement, and be guided by the instructions provided.
- ❖ Assist local law enforcement with locating and identifying possible suspect(s).
- ❖ Secure the emergency information from administrative files and notify the parent(s) and/or guardian(s).

❖ Turn over possible evidence to local law enforcement, who will conduct a further investigation.

❖ Make post notifications to the administrator, additional personnel, and/or departments, per the recommendation of local law enforcement.

❖ Document and collect detailed notes of the incident, which may be used in court as future testimony.

❖ Complete necessary incident report(s).

SUICIDES

Unfortunately suicide is the third leading cause of death among teens age 15-19 (NCSL, 2005), and certainly has an adverse affect on educational institutions, the victim's family, and the community at large. Suicide is often associated with depression, which may be caused by bullying, alcohol or substance abuse, poor social skills, failure and disappointment, and personal-social stress. Since schools can be the first line of defense in reducing the risk of suicide, administrators are in dire need of tools and procedures to address the many concerns if/when a student is in a state of crisis.

If a suicide attempt is threatened, the following procedure is recommended:

❖ Verify the problem, evaluate the findings and take the threat seriously.

❖ Contact 911, local law enforcement, the school administrator, the Safety/Security Department, and the National Institute of Mental Health (NIMH).

❖ Personally speak with the student and reassure him/her that the school cares for their wellbeing.

❖ The school administrator will contact the parent(s) and/or guardian(s) and summon them to the school.

❖ Keep the suicidal student calm, and attempt to isolate him/her.

❖ Make sure the student is never left alone.

❖ After local law enforcement arrives, provide them with all the necessary information.

❖ Provide parents with a list of available counseling resources.

❖ Make sure the student's medical history is available, if requested.

❖ Implement post incident counseling procedures for student body, staff, and/or faculty.

❖ Make post notifications to the senior school administrator, district psychologist, additional personnel, and/or departments, per recommendation of local law enforcement.

❖ Document and collect detailed notes of the incident.

❖ Complete necessary incident report(s).

If a suicide is actually attempted, the following procedure is recommended:

❖ Verify the problem and evaluate your findings.

❖ Contact 911, local law enforcement, the school administrator, Safety/Security Department, and the Emergency Medical Service (EMS).

❖ Keep the suicidal student and all others calm.

❖ In an attempt to neutralize the problem, ask the suicidal student to allow other students to leave the area.

❖ Secure emergency information from the administrative files, and notify parent(s) and/or guardian(s).

❖ Assist local law enforcement with details, and provide assistance if requested to identify possible witnesses or additional victim(s).

❖ Make post notifications to additional personnel and/or departments, per recommendation of local law enforcement.

❖ Be careful not to mention the details of the suicide when notifying family members.

❖ Local law enforcement will handle disclosures after the investigation.

❖ Implement post incident counseling procedures for students, staff, and administrators, if requested.

❖ Make post notifications to the senior school administrator and district psychologist.

- ❖ Document and collect detailed notes of the incident.
- ❖ Complete necessary incident report(s).

If a suicide attempt resulted in death:

- ❖ Follow procedures listed under "Critical Injury/Death/Poisoning – If a death or homicide occurs."

SEVERE WEATHER

Severe weather such as tornados, hurricanes, high winds, cyclones, blizzards, thunderstorms, snowstorms, ice storms, dust storms, and flash floods, occur around the world more frequently than ever before. The National Weather Service and Civil Defense issues warnings for such threats, accompanied by an audible siren and radio or television broadcast. To alert those on or near school property, the following procedure is recommended:

- ❖ Stay abreast of early warning weather conditions.
- ❖ Ensure that the school administrator or principal and Safety/ Security Department are on notice.
- ❖ Monitor alert stations such as Alert Weather Services, Inc., National Oceanic and Atmospheric Administration (NOAA), Weather Stations and the National Weather Service. Weather computer software is also available through Storm Alert, Inc.
- ❖ After the alert signal, take cover inside the nearest building and if time permits, proceed to the lowest level of the facility. Otherwise, take cover in an inner room, hallway or closet.
- ❖ Keep a safe distance from windows and objects that can easily become airborne in high winds.
- ❖ Avoid outside walls, gymnasiums, auditoriums, and other large open areas.
- ❖ If outside and there is no time to move inside, lie down on the ground in a curled position or kneel in a duck-and-cover position. If available, hang onto a fixed object.
- ❖ Class attendance rosters should be used to account for all students.
- ❖ Remain in a secured location until an "all clear" announcement is received.

EARTHQUAKE

Earthquakes and the aftermath can be very challenging events to manage, depending upon the scope of the damage. No one can rightly predict when or where an earthquake will occur, unlike other severe storms, there is no warning signal issued prior to an earthquake. Therefore, being prepared beforehand can greatly reduce the trauma, and other significant issues associated with natural disasters. In the event of an earthquake, the following procedures are recommended:

- ❖ Try to stay calm and take cover.
- ❖ Stay clear of windows, electrical and heating systems, and gas lines.
- ❖ Secure a duck-and-cover position under a desk, table, or bench.
- ❖ Interior halls, archways, standing against an inside wall and doorways, are additional areas suitable for cover.
- ❖ Do not move until the quake has ceased.
- ❖ Do not use elevators.

After the Earthquake, the following procedure is recommended:

- ❖ If there is no physical damage, evacuate the facility.
- ❖ Tune in an emergency station with a portable radio.
- ❖ Keep all students and staff calm, and move everyone to a safe area away from existing buildings.
- ❖ Stay clear of downed wires, and brace for possible aftershocks.
- ❖ Contact school administrators and Safety/Security Department for updates.
- ❖ Class attendance rosters should be used to account for all students.
- ❖ If injuries occurred, administer first aid and contact the Emergency Medical Service (EMS).
- ❖ Do not enter any building until declared safe by proper municipal authorities.
- ❖ Wear protective clothing, and clean areas of debris and spills.

❖ Inspect utilities such as electrical systems, gas lines, sewage and water systems.

❖ Implement post incident counseling procedures for students, staff, and administrators, if requested.

14 EXECUTIVE PROTECTION

Executive Protection (EP) is defined as activities designed to maintain the safety, security, and health of a human asset. EP includes counter measures against "kidnapping", "extortion", and "terrorism"; and is widely utilized by celebrities and "VIPs" (very important persons), to provide personal protection (formerly called bodyguards). The essential components of an EP program are divided into three approaches, risk (threat) assessment, advance procedures, and protective operations (Ortmeier, 2009), and are detailed below:

- ❖ **Risk Assessment** - assists in determining the probability and impact of loss, as well as matching security with threats in order to minimize risk.
- ❖ **Advance Procedures** – the advance is conducted to gather important information about a principal's activities (travel route, destination, meetings, social events, lodging, etc.). The advance includes coordination of the prior, current, and subsequent security arrangements, and bears the responsibility of risk abatement.
- ❖ **Protective Operations** - the mission is to act as an escort to the principal, to provide physical security, and to engage in countermeasures and defensive tactics if necessary (Gip, 2007).

Executive protection team

KIDNAPPING

Kidnapping has become a profitable industry in some countries, and a pattern of kidnapping by terrorists is developing in others. In 1996, a Sanyo executive was kidnapped in Tijuana, Mexico, and subsequently released after a $2 million ransom was paid. In 1999, a Chinese-born executive was also kidnapped in Tijuana and held for a $1 million ransom until he was rescued by Baja California state law enforcement. The possibility of being kidnapped is a frightening thought, and the magnitude of actually becoming a victim is for some, completely overwhelming. The common victim responses of fear, denial, and withdrawal are all experienced in varying degrees. The victim may be blindfolded, handled roughly, stuffed into the trunk of a vehicle, or worse yet, even drugged. If drugs are administered, resistance is inadvisable. The primary use of drugs is to sedate a kidnapping victim and make him/her more manageable; however, being drugged may actually help the victim gain control of their emotions, which would be the immediate goal (The United States State Department, 2008).

If a kidnapping occurs, the following behavior for the victim is suggested:

- ❖ If conscious, follow the captor(s') instructions.
- ❖ Do not antagonize the captor(s). Use brains not brawn.
- ❖ Attempt to stay calm and alert, and try to regain composure as soon as possible to organize personal thoughts.
- ❖ Do not discuss rescue proposals or compliance with ransom demands.
- ❖ Try to establish a rapport with the captor(s). Family is a universal subject. Avoid political dialogues, but listen attentively to the captor(s') point of view. If the language of the captor(s) is known, listen and observe; and if addressed, use it.
- ❖ Plan on a lengthy stay, and determine to keep track of the passage of time. Captor(s) may attempt to confuse the victim's sense of time by taking away a watch, utilizing a windowless cell, or serving meals at odd hours.
- ❖ Approximate time by noting changes in temperatures between night and day, and the frequency and intensity of outside noises (traffic, birds, etc.).
- ❖ Take note of the characteristics of the captor(s) and surroundings: habits, speech, contacts, and other distinctive sounds.
- ❖ Maintain personal dignity and self-respect at all times.
- ❖ Manage time by setting up schedules for simple tasks, exercises, daydreaming, and tidiness.
- ❖ Maintain physical and mental wellbeing, in that it is critical to exercise body and mind.
- ❖ Eat food provided without complaint, which will help maintain strength. Request medical treatment or special medicines if required.
- ❖ Establish exercise and relaxation programs. Exercise produces a healthy tiredness and provides a sense of accomplishment. If

space is confined, do isometrics, as relaxation reduces stress. Techniques include meditation, prayer, and daydreaming. Keep mentally active; read everything and anything available.

❖ Write, even if not allowed to keep the writings. If writing materials are not available, mentally compose poetry, songs or fiction, try to recall Scripture, design structures, and even play games that will assist with stimulation.

EXTORTION

Extortion is defined as blackmail, or theft by intimidation, and involves withholding or obtaining property of another through the threat of some future harm (Ortmeier, 2009). Extortion can be committed through threats of humiliation or exposure of some embarrassing situation, as well as violence, and abuses of authority. For example, a law enforcement official can abuse his/her authority by demanding money or services in lieu of being cited for a traffic violation. Moreover, a politician or public official can be threatened with exposure of past criminal involvement if certain legislation is not passed. In the entertainment community, celebrities can be manipulated by an aggressor to produce large sums of cash by the threat that a loved one will be harmed.

To reduce the chances of being targeted for extortion, the following actions are suggested:

❖ Be a less likely target by avoiding extravagant clothing and jewelry.
❖ Be alert after all banking and ATM transactions.
❖ Be alert to your surroundings, especially after dark, or if you are alone.
❖ Attempt to travel with a companion, and avoid responsive conversation from people you do not know.
❖ Always check the interior of a vehicle prior to entering.
❖ Always lock motor vehicles after entering or exiting.
❖ Contact local law enforcement, a private investigator, or an attorney of any suspicious actions.
❖ Shrink the size of personal estates by dividing assets into smaller limited liability corporations (LLC's).

❖ Avoid directly owning valuable assets.

TERRORISM

Lastly, no security program is complete without addressing the subject of terrorism. Following the September 11, 2001 terrorist attacks on the Pentagon and the World Trade Center, the protection of Americans became a major concern of the Department of Justice (Schmalleger, 2007).

When faced with the possibility of serious harm or death, extreme emotions are provoked, which allow terrorists to succeed. Therefore, to combat terrorism, major initiatives must be continually brought to the forefront. Initiatives include providing local, state and federal law officers with the necessary tools to combat crimes that might be connected with terrorism, i.e., drug trafficking, gang violence, illicit arms trade such as small arms and light weapons, and money laundering. There must also be continual intelligence gathering regarding terrorist cells and fringe groups that may be engaged in the manufacture of nuclear, chemical, biological, radiological weaponry and other potentially deadly materials.

Police special response team

15 CONCLUSION

Throughout the age of modern society, there has been no lack of various methods, strategies, and schools of thought about crime prevention; however, none have had a significant impact with regard to decreasing crime and criminal behavior. Additionally, history has revealed that the fear of crime has had far more of an effect on the quality of life than the actual incidence of crime. In fact, an interesting commentary is that because of fear, people are less likely to become victims of crime because they are limiting activities that could prove to be risky. Of course, by so doing, a false sense of security is being cultivated.

Although crime occurs in any society, the strategic application of the principles and best practices outlined in this handbook, can reduce the incidence of crime, and establish a safer environment. The character Klaatu, in the feature film "The Day the Earth Stood Still", put it best when making the following statement, "There must be security for all, or no one is secure."

DISCLAIMER: The information contained in this handbook, illustrated strategies, techniques and tips, which can be useful to security professionals, architects, and builders. However, care should be taken when applying said principles to specific communities of concern. The material is not meant to serve as an end-all be-all guide to remedy every security problem. In instances where the strategies contained in this handbook conflict with local laws and ordinances, the local governments shall prevail. The author has made all reasonable efforts to provide current and accurate information for the readers of this handbook, and will not be held liable for any unintentional errors or omissions that may be found.

ABOUT THE AUTHOR

Clinton W. Kirkwood Jr. currently serves as a Criminal Justice teacher/ instructor at Canyon and Villa Park High Schools, and Adjunct Professor at Argosy University in Orange County, California. Clint previously served as the Criminal Justice Program Director at ITT-Technical Institute and Westwood College – Anaheim, CA.

The most exciting aspect of Clint's career was his time spent as a police executive with the Detroit Police Department. He retired as the Commanding Officer of the Vice Section/ Narcotics Division, after more than 28 years with the Department. After retiring, he served as Campus Safety Director at Marygrove College in Detroit, and later held a position with AT&T, as the Area Security Manager covering the state of Michigan.

Clint holds a Master of Science degree in Security Administration and a Bachelor of Science degree in Criminal Justice from the University of Detroit Mercy. Clint is a Vietnam veteran who served in the United States Air Force. He currently resides in Yorba Linda, CA with his wife and business partner, Myrah.

REFERENCES

American Society for Industrial Security. (1998). *ASIS International presents introduction to security for business students.* Alexandria, VA: American Society for Industrial Security.

Baker, D. (2007). *Homeownership: the fast path to poverty.* Truthout/ Perspective. Charlotte, NC.

Barren, J. R. (2011). *Executive Protection.* PowerPoint Presentation. Detroit, MI. Jan. 20.

Brea California Police Department. (2011). *Investigations division.* [Online]. Available: ci.brea.ca.us.

Canadian Centre for Occupational Health & Safety. [Online]. Available: ccohs.ca.

Crow, T. D. (2000). *Crime prevention through environmental design* (2nd ed.). Woburn, MA: Butterworth-Heinemann.

Durham City and County Private Sector Task Force. (1996-2010). *Crime prevention through environmental design principles.* [Online]. Available: durham-nc.com.

Federal Emergency Management Agency. (2007). *Welcome to the national incident management system integration center.* [Online]. Available: fema.gov.

Gips, M. A. (2007). *Security Management: My short life as an EP specialist.*

Grand Junction Police Department Community Advocacy Program. (2010). *Neighborhood watch program.* [Online]. Available: gjcity. org.

Heriot-Watt University, Edinburgh, Scotland. (2004). *the built environment.* [Online]. Available: sbe.hw.ac.uk

International Association of Chiefs of Police. (2000). *Private sector liaison committee.* Alexandria, VA.

Marygrove College. (1999). *Campus safety disaster preparedness plan.* Detroit, MI.

Menasha, WI Police Department. *Chronic nuisance program.* [Online]. Available: town-menasha.com.

National Conference of State Legislatures. (2005). *State Health Lawmakers Digest: Teen suicide prevention.* Volume 5, Number 5.

National League of Cities. (2008). *Mortgage foreclosures: police-community response.* [Online]. Available: api.ning.com.

Newman, O. (1976). *Design guidelines for creating defensible space.* Washington, DC: Law Enforcement Assistance Administration.

Oliver, W. M. (2007). *Homeland security for policing.* Upper Saddle River, NJ: Pearson Prentice Hall.

Ortmeier, P. J. (2009). *Introduction to security: operations and management (3rd ed.).* Upper Saddle River, NJ: Pearson Prentice Hall.

Pence, K. (2008). *Homeownership and mortgage initiatives.* Synopses of Selected Research on Housing, Mortgages, and Foreclosures.

Prince William County Police Department, Special Operations Bureau. *Crime Prevention-CPTED.* [Online]. Available: pwcgov.org.

Public Safety and Homeland Security Bureau. *Federal communications commission.* [Online]. Available: transition.fcc.gov.

Schmalleger, F. (2007). *Criminal Justice Today (9th ed.).* Upper Saddle River, NJ: Pearson Prentice Hall.

Sennewald, C. A. (2003). *Effective security management (4th ed.).* Boston, MA: Butterworth-Heinemann.

Sorensen, S. L. (2000). *Crime prevention through environmental design.* ConsultingCorporation, Los Angeles, CA.

United State Department of Homeland Security. *Federal emergency management agency.* [Online]. Available: fema.gov.

United States Department of Housing and Urban Development. (1996). *National crime institute crime prevention brief.* Washington, DC: U.S. Government Printing Office.

United States Department of Labor. (2010). *Bureau of labor statistics.* [Online]. Available: bls.gov.

United States National Library of Medicine. (2009). *National institute of health.* [Online]. Available: nlm.nih.gov.

United States State Department. (2008). *Kidnapping*. [Online]. Available: Department of State Publication 10217.

Utah Department of Public Safety. *Office of emergency service*. [Online]. Available: publicsafety.utah.gov.

Walsh, T. J., & Healy, R. J. (1997). *Protection of assets manual*. Santa Monica, CA: The Merritt Company.

PHOTO COURTESY

alaska.fws.gov *(defensible space)*
belson.com *(bus stop shelter)*
cinl.com *(industrial building parking)*
energysavers.gov *(lighting)*
energysavers.gov *(tables)*
hacla.org *(public housing)- courtesy of the Housing Authority of the City of Los Angeles*
hgrostudio.com *(book cover)*
sdl@street-design.com *(planters as natural surveillance)*
tessellarsociety.blogspot.com *(housing area with single entrance)*
thinkstock.com *(access control with cctv)*
thinkstock.com *(architectural drawing)*
thinkstock.com *(bench & park signage)*
thinkstock.com *(broken window theory)*
thinkstock.com *(building with hardened security features)*
thinkstock.com *(commercial buildings serve as additional eyes & ears)*
thinkstock.com *(commercial building with hardened security)*
thinkstock.com *(chain-link fence)*
thinkstock.com *(cop tower)*
thinkstock.com *(cpted concept)*
thinkstock.com *(cpted landscaping)*
thinkstock.com *(emergency phones)*
thinkstock.com *(gateway & traffic calming intersection)*
thinkstock.com *(home with proper night lighting)*
thinkstock.com *(landscaping)*
thinkstock.com *(lighting with security cam)*
thinkstock.com *(low-level landscaping design)*

thinkstock.com *(neighborhood watch)*
thinkstock.com *(neighboring businesses - partnerships)*
thinkstock.com *(open & highly visible play area))*
thinkstock.com *(parking structure with openings)*
thinkstock.com *(police special response team)*
thinkstock.com *(proper landscaping maintenance)*
thinkstock.com *(properly maintained parking facility)*
thinkstock.com *(self-service bank & atm from road))*
thinkstock.com *(signage)*
thinkstock.com *(space ownership defined)*
thinkstock.com *(well defined property)*
urbanthinker.com *(play area)*